Table of Contents
For cross reference in the
NCATT AET Test Study Guide

Chapter 3 – Semiconductors

NCATT AET TEST
Worksheet Book

Bruce Bessette

Cover design BCS.LLC
www.bessetteaviationconsulting.com
ISBN-13:
978-1497359673
ISBN-10:
1497359678

Chapter 4 – Electrical Storage, Analog and Logic Switching

Chapter 5 – Aircraft Wire and Blue Prints

Chapter 6 Aviation Workplace Safety

Chapter 7 Aircraft Construction, Performance and System Troubleshooting

Index of Worksheets

How to use this book

As a part of the test review course I teach all over the country and at my home school I used worksheet to help with study. The original course was 2 and 1/2 hours a day, 5 days a week for 5 weeks. This allowed for plenty of time for class work and review. Now that my review course is now 36 contact hours the worksheets are more important than ever. But for a reason I will explain I had to control how this book is intended to be used.

When I made the book available for sale to the public, hoped that it would be used with the textbook as a study package. However some people were buying just the workbook alone and attempting to memorized the questions or make flash cards to prepare for the test. I even found some flash cards from the worksheet book on the internet. Now I have no problem with the flash cards or that they used my book to generate them. None of the information in my book is super-secret. I just took information that was found in at least 5 textbook sources and package them into a study package for a test I studied, reviewed and interview test takers for.

The issue I have is that the NCATT AET test is unpublished and I do not know the exact questions that people can memorize. You need to be able to answer the questions by learning the material. If you try memorizing answers you more than likely not pass. Another problem for memorizing test takers is that the formats of the questions are different than the review format that this worksheet book is designed.

To review all of the subject areas in the test I needed to section the material in small bites. To help speed up the review for some the short subject format allows for some to skip material that they already know. Some of the actual test questions on the NCATT AET test require intuitive thinking that requires the technician to create a solution from the information provided in the context of the question. Some people complain that the questions are tricky and unfair. However when I ask them to give me the actual context of the question we both discover that all of the information was there to answer the question was there.

I really suggest to everyone that they purchase the worksheet books with the textbook and challenge themselves to answer at least every other question. If you have trouble then go back over the textbook and review or even go to the original FAA A&P 8083-30 and other government sources where the review information is collected from. Remember the textbook and the worksheet book is designed to provide information for a review of material you have already seen. The benefit of the textbook is that it is one source reading for all 34 subject areas in the AET test. The NCATT AET requires that you have an FAA Airframe and Powerplant Certificate, some experience in working in industrial settings and have knowledge of radio and logic circuits. This book was written to provide a review of information in the test. If you have not ever seen some subject in this book then you will need to learn that subject using more complete material or take an basic electricity course online.

For the investment of $350 dollars you will have something to open doors into the world of Aircraft Avionics Maintenance. But like every certificate a technician obtains, that certificate is a license to learn. From here go on and earn your NCATT additional ratings certification. Just like the FAA A&P certificate the Generals portion of the test for mechanics is designed to test general subjects in aircraft maintenance. The AET is designed to certify that at technician is knowledgeable in general avionics. The next step is to certify your ability to understand more complex avionics systems. NCATT has currently four additional ratings:

Radio Communications Systems: (RCS) This subject covers basic radio system operation to include VHF Communications, Radio Wave, Radio modulation, Audio Selection, Line Replaceable Units and antennas.

Dependent Navigation Systems (DNS): These cover navigation systems that require reception from a ground station. These system include Automatic Direction Finding, VOR, ILS and GPS systems.

Onboard Communications and Safety Systems (OCS): This subject covers aircraft internal aircraft communications like the Service Interphone system and the aircraft PA systems. This certification includes Satellite and WiFi systems and Data Recording for Voice and Flight.

Autonomous Navigation Systems: (ANS): This standard is for systems in the aircraft that help the pilot navigate and fly. From the aircrafts attitude and compass system to modern Heading and Attitude systems found in AHRS and ADIRU.

NCATT has plans for two new certifications for avionics are the Flight Management Systems and Auto flight systems. Information for the additional ratings can be found in my Avionics Technician Handbooks. These two books cover everything from the basic flight instruments and engine indicating systems to systems in the radios center stack and communications and navigation systems. Information for these, other books and courses for avionics can be found on;

www.bessetteaviationconsulting.com

Worksheet 1
Chapter 1, Section 1

Basic DC Electrical Terms

Answer in complete sentences.

1. What part of an atom is associated with the flow of electricity?

2. What in electrons in a conductor determines whether its flow is poor or good?

3. Define Static Electricity?

4. What term is used to express the flow of electricity?

5. Define Coulomb.

6. What is the basic unit of electrical pressure? What other names could it go by?

7. If voltage and resistance are known, describe how total current can be determined. Show the equation.

8. What device other than an actual battery can be used to store energy?

9. Describe the left hand rule as it pertains to electrical generation.

10. What trait would allow magnetic lines of flux to flow easily?

11. Describe the name of a common electrical point that allows circuits to have a return path to power?

12. What will have the effect of slowing current a large of small amount of resistance?

13. Describe the electrical relationship of voltage, current and resistance described in Ohms Law.

14. How much work can be achieved with one watts of energy?

15. Describe what current does in a series circuit?

16. How is voltage distributed in a parallel circuit?

17. Describe the rule for current and magnetism for the left hand rule for generators.

18. What large difference of electrical potential has no useful purpose in aviation?

19. What is the property called when lines of magnetic flux travel freely through a material?

20. What is the basic unit of measure for a capacitor?

21. Which type of battery cannot be recharge in a circuit?

Worksheet 2
Chapter 1, Section 2

Resistors and Resistance

Answer in complete sentences or draw the electrical symbol.

1. Draw a Symbol for a standard resistor.

2. Describe the ways a resistor can be identified.

3. What are some types of variable resistors?

4. What is/are the purpose/s of a resistor in a circuit?

5. In the four color band system of resistor identification, what is the third color band represent?

6. Which resistors cannot apply to Ohms Law?

7. What is meant by the term tolerances as it refers to the fourth color band?

Using the four color code, determine the value of the following resistors.

8. Black   Green   Black   Gold

9. Blue   Red   Orange   Silver

10. Brown   Brown   Black   NC

11. White   Black   Yellow   Silver

12. How can resistors wattage capability be determine by looking at it?

Worksheet 3
Chapter 1, Section 3

Ohms Law

1. Define Ohms Law in the relationship of voltage to current and resistance.

2. Define Ohms Law for the relationship of current to voltage and resistance.

3. Define Ohms Law for the relationship of resistance to voltage and current.

4. Using Ohms Laws, solve for voltage when given current as 2 amps to the resistance of 5 Ohms. Also write out your formula

5. Solve for unknown current when given the voltage is 12 volts and the resistance is 6 Ω, show your formula.

6. Solve for Resistance when given the voltage is 120Vdc and the current is 60A, show your formula.

7. What is the relationship of power to voltage and current, write out the formula?

8. How much power is being produced in a circuit when the measured current is 60 amps and the applied voltage is 110 volts?

Worksheet 4
Chapter 1, Section 4

Circuit Voltage Reading

1. Define what is a reference point in a circuit?

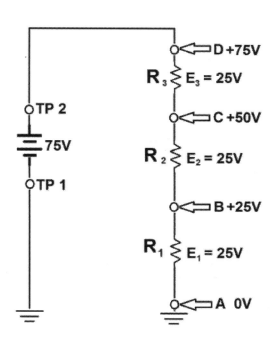

2. For the circuit on the right what is the rule for voltage?

3. What is the rule about current in the diagram at right?

4. Refer to the diagram, what is the voltage drop across point B and D?

5. What is the voltage drop across point A and TP 1?

6. What is the voltage drop across point A and D?

7. What is the voltage drop between point B and TP 1?

Worksheet 5
Chapter 1, Section 5

Series Circuit Calculations for Resistors

1. What is the rule for calculation of total resistance for series circuits?

2. What is the rule for current in a series circuit?

3. What is the rule of voltage in a series circuit?

4. Refer to the diagram at right what is the total resistance?

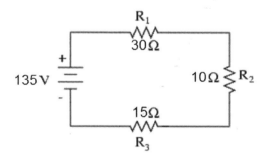

5. Using the same diagram at right, what is the total current?

6. What is the voltage drop across R_2?

7. For the circuit at right, what is the total voltage applied?

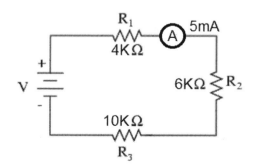

8. What is the voltage drop across R_3?

Worksheet 6
Chapter 1, Section 5

Parallel Circuit Calculations for Resistors

1. What is the rule for voltage distribution in a parallel circuit?

2. What is the rule for current paths in a parallel circuit?

3. What is the rule for total resistance in a parallel circuit?

4. Refer to the diagram at right and solve for total resistance.

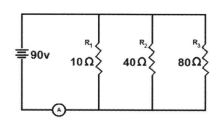

5. Using the product over sum method solve for the total resistance for the diagram at right.

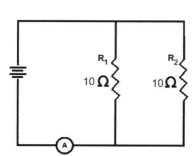

6. Using the diagram at right determine the total resistance using the equal branches method.

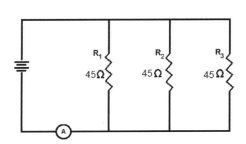

7. Refer to the diagram at right and solve for the total current to the V_S.

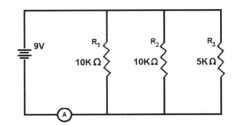

8. Using the diagram at right and determine the following.

R_T =

I_T =

E_{R1} =

I_{R1} =

E_{R2} =

I_{R2} =

E_{R3} =

I_{R3} =

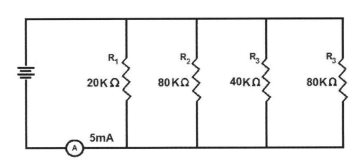

Worksheet 7
Chapter 1, Section 5

Series/Parallel Circuit Calculations for Resistors

1. Refer to the diagram at right and determine the following.

   R_T =

   E_T =

   E_{R1} =

   E_{R2} =

   E_{R3} =

   I_{R1} =

   I_{R2} =

   I_{R3} =

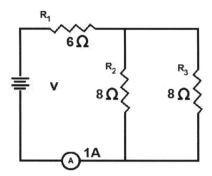

2. Refer to the diagram at right and determine the following.

   R_T =

   E_T =

   E_{R1} =

   E_{R2} =

   E_{R3} =

   E_{R4} =

   E_{R5} =

   E_{R6} =

   E_{R7} =

   I_{R1} =

   I_{R2} =

   I_{R3} =

   I_{R4} =

   I_{R5} =

   I_{R6} =

   I_{R7} =

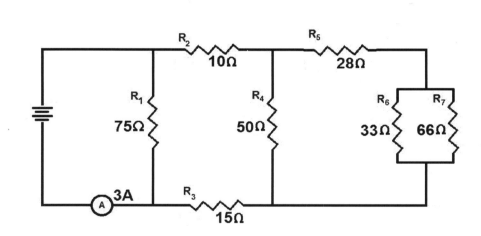

Worksheet 8
Chapter 2, Section 1

AC Terms

1. Define Alternating Current.

2. What is frequency?

3. What is the unit of measure for AC frequency?

4. What is the measure of a Hz?

5. What is the resistance to current flow that can exist in an AC circuit?

6. What is a part of electrical impedance to AC when compared to electrical properties of capacitors and inductors?

7. What is the opposition of current flow that is produced by a capacitor?

8. What is the phase relationship in a capacitance circuit between current and voltage?

9. Draw out the mathematical formula for Capacitive Reactance.

10. What is the current to voltage relationship in a purely inductive circuit?

11. What is the mathematical formula you would use to determine Inductive Reactance?

12. How is a sine wave plotted?

13. In a sine wave at what plot or position of the magnetic field is the current and voltage are at maximum values?

14. What is the effective value of power of an AC voltage when compared to a DC voltage?

15. How peak voltage calculated for an AC signal?

16. What is the measure between two or more signals that are not perfectly timed to each other?

17. What is the measure of a ratio of power dissipated over the power inputted into the circuit?

18. What is the phantom power that is expended in a circuit due to the energy expended by capacitors and inductors?

19. For three phase motors winding methods, which method of motor winding has all of the lows connected to a common point?

20. What is a three phase motor also known as, when discribing the output signal waveform?

21. What device converts an AC signal into a type of DC output?

22. What electrical device will convert a DC input into a type of AC output?

23. What is it called when a meter is placed between the voltage source and load and a reduction is measured?

24. What is being described when an algebraic sum of current flowing away from a single point is equal to the sum of all current flowing to that same point?

25. What is a device that splits current flow into two paths for the purpose of taking a measurement between the two paths?

Worksheet 9
Chapter 2, Section 2

Generating Electrical Power

1. What is the device called that produces the flow of current by mechanically passing a conductor through a magnetic field?

2. What are the two possible voltage types that can be produced by generators?

3. What is the purpose of a commutator in an electric motor?

4. What is the sine wave output of a single conductor generator with brushes and commutator as it rotates?

5. What are some problems or hazards around DC motors and generators have that AC generator don't normally have especially at high altitudes?

6. What determines the output frequency of an AC generator?

7. Refer to the diagram at right, what type of generator would produce a sine wave like this?

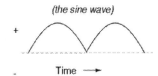

(the sine wave)

Time

Worksheet 10
Chapter 2, Section 3

AC Voltage Waveform

1. Describe what is a cycle of AC voltage?

2. What is the unit of measurement for frequency?

3. What is the formula for the determination of frequency?

4. What device is used to plot the graphical representation of the sine wave?

5. Other than the sine wave, name three other types of electrical waveforms.

6. How would the frequency 123.00MHz be rewritten out in words?

7. If time or rate of wave form is frequency, how is the amplitude of an AC signal measured?

8. What is the total height of amplitude in an AC waveform called?

9. What is the total true average voltage for an AC waveform?

10. When measuring the equivalent power output of an AC waveform to a comparable DC power output, what term is used to describe the AC measurement?

11. How is RMS determined in an AC waveform?

12. With a peak voltage of 12vAC, what is the effective value for this voltage?

Worksheet 11
Chapter 2, Section 4

Simple AC circuit calculations

1. Are resistors calculated differently in an AC circuit when compared to an equivalent DC one, why or why not?

2. What is the rule to remember when calculating the AC voltages in your final circuit outcome?

3. When a schematic has an AC signal input, what is the symbol?

4. What other forms of resistance can be produced in an AC circuit?

5. Which types of components create reactance in an AC circuit?

Worksheet 12
Chapter 2, Section 5

AC Phase

1. Define phase as it refers to the timing of two AC signals?

2. How are phases of waveforms measured against each other?

3. At what phase would two signals exactly cancel each other out?

4. For the diagram below, describe the relationship between A and B.

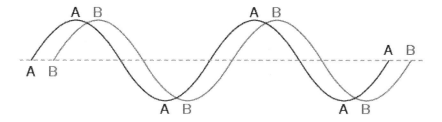

Worksheet 13
Chapter 2, Section 6

RCL Circuits

1. Define what is an RCL circuit is.

2. For what type of signal can an RCL circuit pass current through all of its components?

3. In an RCL circuit what is the unit of measure of resistance that each component produces?

4. What is the resistance to current flow that is caused by the inductor and the capacitor?

5. What is the phase relationship between the impedance from the capacitor and inductor?

6. What is the phase relationship from the applied voltage and the resistor?

7. What is the unit of measure for an inductor in a circuit?

8. What is the resistance to current flow caused by an inductor in an AC circuit called?

9. In a circuit that contains an inductor, how does the inductor affect current flow when current is first applied?

10. What four factors affect the capacity of an inductor?

11. What is the purpose of using a high permeability core in an inductor?

12. What are the two electrical properties of a capacitor?

13. How is a capacitor electrically different than a battery?

14. What is the unit of measure of a capacitor?

15. What is the physical construction of a capacitor?

16. Describe what Reactance is in an AC circuit and what is the unit of measure?

17. What types of reactance is there in an RCL circuit and what are the symbols for each?

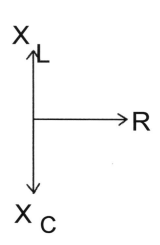

18. Refer to the graph at right and describe the circuit if the reactance plot is straight up (X>0)

19. What is the mathematical formula for X_L?

20. Solve for X_L when: Frequency =400Hz and Inductor = 60H

21. Solve for X_L when: Frequency =60KHz and Inductor = 20mH

Worksheet 14
Chapter 2, Section 6

Computing Total Inductance

1. How is inductive reactance in a series circuit computed?

2. When given a circuit where you have the values of the inductors and the frequency of the input, how would you determine the Total Reactance in the circuit?

3. Refer to the diagram at right and solve for the Total Reactance in the circuit. (X_{LT})

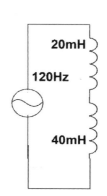

4. Refer to the diagram at right and solve for Total Reactance in the circuit. (X_{LT})

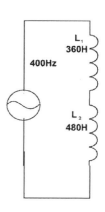

5. How is Total Inductive Reactance determined in a parallel circuit?

6. Refer to the diagram at right and determine the total X_{LT} in the circuit.

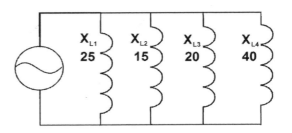

7. What is Mutual Inductance?

8. What are the two parts of a coil called in the Mutual Induction process?

9. Is the current and voltage always in phase between the primary and the secondary?

Worksheet 15
Chapter 2, Section 6

Capacitance Reactance

1. Refer to the graph at the right, what is the circuit plot when the circuit is down?

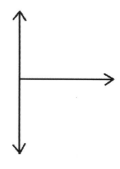

2. Write out the mathematical formula for X_C.

3. What is the mathematical relationship between frequency and capacitance to Capacitive Reactance?

4. Determine the X_C when: 2µF Capacitor and input of 50Hz

5. Determine the X_C when: 5µF Capacitor and input of 120Hz

6. What is the formula for X_{CT} for capacitors in a series circuit?

7. Determine the X_{CT} for the circuit at the right.

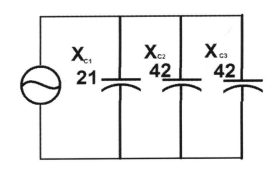

Worksheet 16
Chapter 2, Section 6

Facts about Series RCL Circuits

1. For the RCL waveform plots, what are the two electrical properties being measured?

2. What is the amplitude relationship between the applied voltage and current in an RCL plot?

3. What component is always in phase with the applied voltage and current?

4. What is the maximum amount of phase difference that can exist in an RCL plot?

5. In a series RCL circuit what plot would be common in all of the components?

6. What does the term ELI the ICE man phrase referring to?

7. What is the measure of all of the total resistance to current flow?

8. What is the determination in an RCL circuit when the Z vector is plotted either positive or negative?

9. Determine the Impedance vector when: Resistance 10Ω
   Capacitance 3µF
   Inductance 5H
   Frequency 60Hz

10. Determine the Impedance vector when: Resistance 25Ω
   Capacitance 6pF
   Inductance 2mH
   Frequency 2KHz

Worksheet 17
Chapter 2, Section 6

Facts about Parallel RCL Circuits

1. In a parallel RCL circuit, what is common through all of the components?

2. Using ELI the ICE man, what is the variable for the impedance plot?

3. Refer to the diagram at right and solve for Total Current and Total Impedance.

   $I_T =$

   $Z_T =$

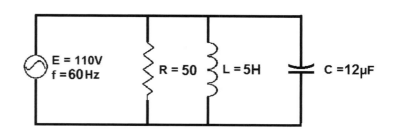

4. Refer to the diagram at right and solve for Total Current and Total Impedance.

   $I_T =$

   $Z_T =$

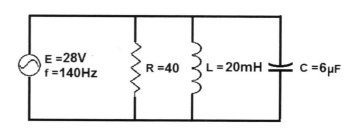

Worksheet 18
Chapter 2, Section 6

Resonant Circuit Operation

1. What is Resonance in a RCL circuit?

2. What variable allows an RCL to operate at Resonance?

3. What two components in a RCL circuit determine the resonance frequency?

4. What is the relationship between current and impedance in a series RCL circuit operating at resonance?

Refer to the diagram at right and answer the following
5. Identify which is the upper H_{PP}

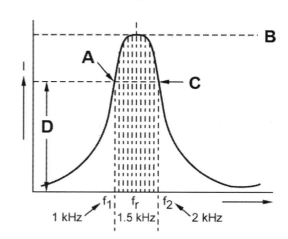

6. What is used to determine the bandwidth in this diagram?

7. What is item D measuring?

8. Given f1 is at 122 MHz and f2 is at 126 MHz, what is the bandwidth of this plot?

9. Determine the Resonance Frequency of an RCL circuit when given:

Capacitor   6µF
Inductor   50mH
Resistor   20Ω

10. Determine the Resonance Frequency of an RCL circuit when given:

Capacitor   15µF
Inductor   10H
Resistor   100KΩ

11. What is Q as it refers to in AC circuit?

12. How is Q classified and identified?

Worksheet 19
Chapter 2, Section 6

Resonance in a Parallel RCL Circuit

1. What is the major operational difference parallel RCL circuits have when operating at resonance when compared to series ones?

2. What is another name that is used for the tank circuits in devices such as oscillators?

3. What is needed to start a tank circuit oscillating?

4. What is happing in a tank circuit that makes it oscillate?

5. What is the action called that occurs in the tank circuit when it is oscillating?

6. If the tank circuit does not receive any new voltage, what will happen to the output signal?

7. For problem #6, what element in the circuit causes the problem with the output signal?

8. What is that signal called that is added to the tank circuit to maintain its output amplitude?

Worksheet 20
Chapter 2, Section 7

Transformer Operation

1. What are the two parts of a transformer?

2. What is the normal purpose of a transformer?

3. When you change voltage, what is proportionality changed in the transformation?

4. Describe what is happing to voltage and current when you have a step down transformer.

5. Given the following information: Primary Voltage – 120 volts, Secondary voltage is 60 volts. What is the transformer ratio and whether this is a step up or step down transformer.

6. What is the input voltage of a 10: 1 transformer when the output is 60Vac?

7. What is the current of the secondary of a 10: 25 transformer when the primary current is 50 amps?

8. What is the ratio of a transformer when the primary voltage is 30 volts and the secondary is 900 volts?

9. What is the output voltage of a transformer with 300 turns in the primary and 900 turns in the secondary with an input voltage of 45 Vac?

Worksheet 21
Chapter 3, Section 1

Semiconductors

1. What are the conducting properties of pure semiconducting material?

2. What process is used to increase the conductibility of the semiconductor material?

3. How is N Type material created during manufacturing?

4. What electrical properties does the P Type material have?

5. Draw a standard P-N Diode and identify the anode and cathode sections.

6. What is meant by the term forward bias in a diode?

7. When voltage is applied to the anode end, what happens electrically to the diode?

Worksheet 22
Chapter 3, Section 2

Diode Operation and Configurations

1. What is the process of an AC signal when it passes a diode?

2. What doped material make up the anode and the cathode segments of a diode?

3. When looking at the physical diode, how do you determine the cathode end?

4. How much forward bias is normally required to get a P-N silicon diode flowing?

5. What is the condition a diode is in when current is forced against the anode?

6. Can a standard silicon based diode operate past breakdown voltage for extended lengths of time?

7. What is a very common use of diodes in electrical circuits?

8. With an input voltage of 5Vac, what is the RMS voltage of the signal past the diode?

Worksheet 23
Chapter 3, Section 3

Rectification

1. Define rectification.

2. For an AC audio signal, why rectify the input?

3. What type of rectifier is a single diode?

4. What type of rectifier is a bridge circuit?

5. Using the space below, draw a diagram of a bridge rectifier and identify the input and output signals.

Power Supply Filters

1. How is the waveform described that comes from a full wave rectifier?

2. In what configuration to the load is a choke filter connected.

3. How is the capacitor connected for it to be used as a signal filter?

4. What is the Choke inductor do to the output of the rectifier?

5. How does the capacitor maintain the higher average signal for the output signal?

6. What is the configuration of a Pi filter?

7. What is the purpose of the bleeder resistor placed at the output?

Worksheet 25
Chapter 3, Section 3

Variactor Diodes

1. What uses are there for a variactor diode?

2. What part of the variactor creates the variable capacitance?

3. In what class of operation is the diode in when operating as a variactor?

4. As the reverse bias voltage decreases what happens to the capacitance value of the variactor?

5. What can happen to a variactor when the reverse bias voltage is increased   above its rated level?

Worksheet 26
Chapter 3, Section 3

Semiconductor Voltage Regulation

1. When a silicon diode is operating in forward bias how much voltage regulation can be achieved per diode?

2. When a diode is operating as a voltage regulator what is its normal operating condition?

3. For the diagram below, what is the purpose of R1?

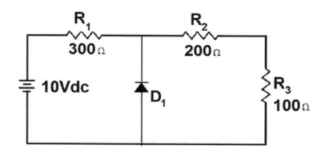

4. In the diagram above, which is the load resistor?

5. When a voltage regulating diode is operating what is created by the diode other than a set voltage?

6. What does a Schottky Diode have over Zener diodes based on the operating principle?

7. Draw a schematic symbol for a Zener and Schottky Diodes.

8. When using a diode as a voltage regulator, what is being measured for the output of the regulator?

9. What is the effective resistance of a diode operating in reverse bias?

10. What is the purpose of a Zener Diode?

11. Refer to the diagram at right and determine the voltage drop across R$_3$?

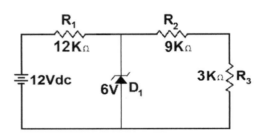

12. What makes a Schottky Diode different from any other type of rectifying diode?

13. What is the main use of a Schottky Diode?

Worksheet 27
Chapter 3, Section 4

Electronic Voltage Regulators

1. For a voltage regulator diode what is the region called in the operating range that provides voltage regulation?

2. How is a diode constructed that allows for different voltages to be regulated and how does a technical determine this?

3. For the diagram below, what is the purpose of the R1 resistor?

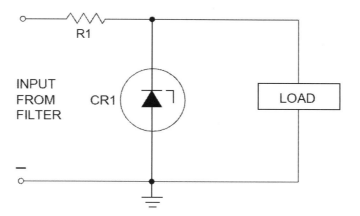

4. For the diagram above what is the total amperes of the circuit with an input voltage of 50 volts, Zener voltage of 28 volts a load resistance of 300Ω and a series resistance of 550Ω?

5. For the diagram above determine the load current?

6. For the diagram in question 4, what is the Zener current with an input voltage of 27 volts?

7. What are the circuit limitations for a shunt Zener diode regulator when more loads are added to the load?

8. What does adding a transistor in series to the load provide for the voltage regulator?

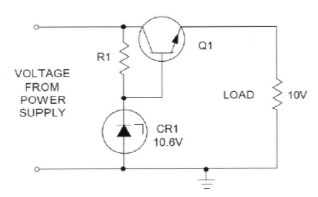

9. Refer to the diagram above, what determines the forward bias of the transistor Q1?

10. For a transistor in a voltage regulator, as the input voltage increases, what happens to the bias of the transistor?

11. Looking at the diagram at right, determine the number of major flows of current.

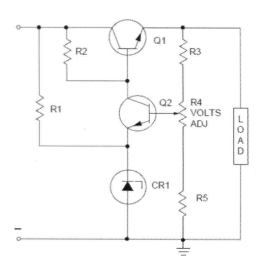

12. Which device in this circuit allows current to flow directly from the load?

13. Which device is the current control for the Zener CR1?

14. When the input voltage is increased in what part of the circuit is the first signal change sensed?

15. When the voltage at the source is decrease and the forward bias at Q2 is decreased, how is the series transistor Q1 changed to adapt to the changes?

16. For the voltage regulator above, in what direction does R4 need to be adjusted to increase the output of the load voltage?

Worksheet 28
Chapter 3, Section 5

Transistors

1. What electrical device did the transistor replace in electrical circuits?

2. Define bipolar junction transistor. (BJT)

3. Refer to the diagram at right and identify the three leads that come out of the transistor.

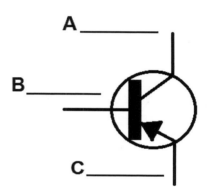

A_____

B_____

C_____

4. Refer to the diagram below, identify the type of junctions.

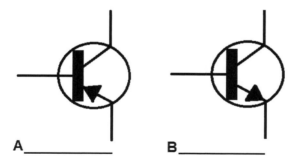

A_____   B_____

5. Refer to the diagram below and draw an arrow indication the current flow through each transistor.

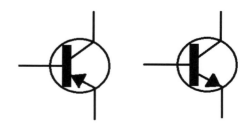

6. What is done during manufacturing of a transistor that determines the current flow through the diode?

7. What are the three conditions that a transistor will operate at?

8. When a transistor is being used as a switch, what two conditions determine the operation?

9. Refer to the diagram below, what is the percentage of current flow through the various junctions of the device?

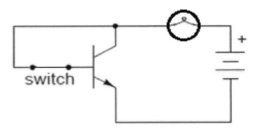

10. Refer to the diagram below, what state is the transistor?

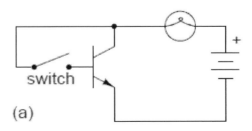

(a)

Worksheet 29
Chapter 3, Section 6

Amplifiers

1. What is the primary purpose of an amplifier?

2. For a standard amplifier what are the basic components?

3. When a DC voltage is applied to the amplifier without an input voltage, what condition are the junctions in the transistor?

4. At what point in the amplifier is the input signal applied?

5. When the signal is applied to BJT, how is the current in the transistor changed?

6. What are the different types of transistors that can be used in amplifiers?

7. What are the connections leads of a field effect transistor (FET) identified in a circuit?

8. What is the main difference in a metal-oxide FETs that differ from pure semiconductor FETs?

9. In a simple amplifier circuit, what analog type component is the transistor in an amplifier working most like?

10. What is the purpose of the resistor placed on the source voltage in an amplifier?

11. How is the signal of a standard amplifier connected to the output?

12. What is the signal gain defined as that is produced by the amplifier?

Worksheet 30
Chapter 3, Section 7

Transistor Configurations of Amps

1. Refer to the three configurations at right, what is the common connection for each configuration that help identify each?

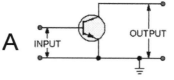

A   INPUT   OUTPUT

2. Refer to the diagram at right and indicate each configuration.

   a. _____

   b. _____

   c. _____

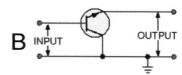

B   INPUT   OUTPUT

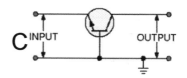

C   INPUT   OUTPUT

3. Define the term bias as it is used in an amplifier circuit?

4. How can bias applied at the base of the transistor affect the operation of the amplifier?

5. In an amplifier what is the phase from the input to the output?

6. For a perfect reproduction of the output waveform what must be present to keep the emitter junction current flowing all of the time.

For the next 7 questions refer to the diagram

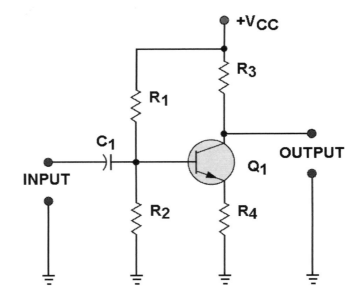

7. Which develops the forward bias of Q1?

8. What is the purpose of C1?

9. What controls the output of the amplifier?

10. What is the phase relationship of the output to the input?

11. What is purpose of the Vcc in this amplifier?

12. What does R4 control or compensate for?

13. What is the configuration of this Amplifier?

Worksheet 31
Chapter 3, Section 7

Static or Quiescent Operation

1. What is meant by a static operation of an amplifier?

2. For the static bias voltage, what is the path where the voltage is applied?

3. What is considered dynamic amplifier operation?

Worksheet 32
Chapter 3, Section 7

Characteristic Curve Graph

1. What is being plotted on an amplifier characteristic graph?

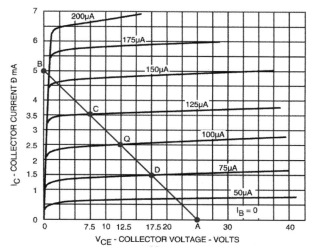

2. What does the line between point A and B determined?

3. How is the cutoff voltage point determined in this graph?

4. How is the saturation point determined?

5. What is the "Q" point on the plot determine?

6. What is gain as it refers to amplifiers?

7. What does bias control in an amplifier circuit?

8. How is the "Q" point determined?

9. What is the proportional relationship between gain and the output of the amplifier?

10. What is the formula for amplifier gain?

11. Which resistor/s changes the collector current which determines the operation of the amplifier between saturation and cutoff?

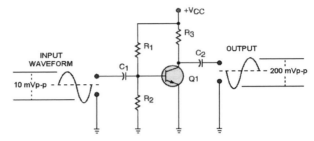

Worksheet 33
Chapter 3, Section 7

Amplifier Classes of Operation

1. What are the four classes of amplifier operation?

2. What are the classes of operation being measured against?

3. Which class of operation gives the best fidelity?

4. Which class of amplifier still gives decent fidelity but preserves power because the collector conducts from 99 to 50 percent of the time?

5. Which class of amplifier is used primarily for power amplification?

6. What type of amplifier is used for impedance matching?

7. For the impedance matching amplifier, what is the gain?

For the next three questions refer to the diagram at right.

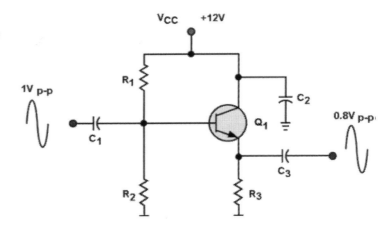

8. What devices determines the forward bias of this amplifier?

9. What is the output gain of this amplifier?

10. What is the useful purpose of this amplifier?

Worksheet 34
Chapter 3, Section 7

Temperature Stabilization

1. What is meant when a device has a negative temperature coefficient?

2. What is the problem in an amplifier that develops when the transistor begins to operate at a lower resistance?

3. Where should the swamping resistor be placed in the circuit for temperature stabilization of an amplifier?

4. What is added to a circuit to help bypass the swamping resistor at lower load conditions?

5. What does the thermistor do at the base input of the transistor do?

6. What in the construction of diodes makes them useful for temperature stabilization in amplifiers?

7. What is the purpose of installing two diodes on the bias for amplifiers?

8. What is a method use to directly removed heat from a transistor in an amplifier?

Worksheet 35
Chapter 3, Section 7

Amplifier Coupling

1. What is the purpose of a cascade amplifier?

2. Which coupling will pass DC?

3. What component causes high frequency gain losses in the coupling?

4. In a LC coupler what controls the gain for that type of amplifier?

5. What type of coupling method has poor low frequency response because of the X_C in the circuit?

6. Which coupling is best when needing to reduce feedback from the amplifier to the load?

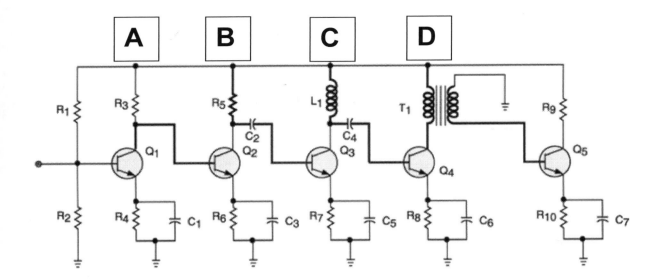

Refer to the diagram and match the letter to the correct coupling type.

7. Transformer_____

8. Direct_____

9. LC _____

10. RC _____

Worksheet 36
Chapter 3, Section 8

Oscillators

1. Before the use of signal modulation how was information broadcasted by radio waves?

2. What is the primary purpose of an oscillator?

3. What are the four main components that make up an oscillator?

4. What are the two stable outputs desired of the oscillator?

5. What component determines the output frequency?

6. What is regenerative feedback loop in an oscillator and what is it achieving in the circuit?

7. Define resonance operation.

Refer to the diagram below, answer the next 7 questions to identify each component in the question.

8. What are the components biasing the output of the amplifier?

9. What is the FDD?

10. What can change the output frequency?

11. What is the regenerative feedback loop?

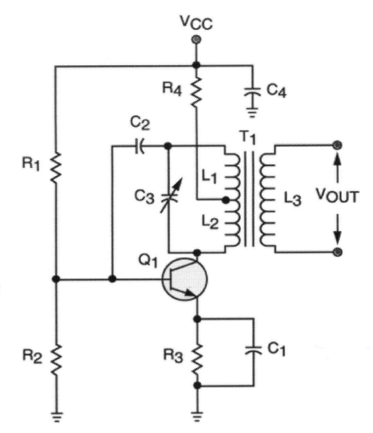

12. What is used for thermal stabilization?

13. What is used to isolate the AC output frequency from the DC power supply?

14. What is the output coupled to?

Worksheet 37
Chapter 3, Section 8

Buffer Amplifiers/ Multipliers

1. What is meant by the term "High Impedance"?

2. How does a buffer amplifier reduce the impedance of the output?

3. What is the gain of a buffer amplifier?

4. What class of amplifier are frequency multipliers?

5. What is occurring to the output waveform when the cutoff bias is very high?

6. What could happen to the harmonic frequencies in a frequency doubler if the output is multiplied too many times?

Worksheet 38
Chapter 3, Section 8

Crystal Controlled Oscillators

1. What is the property of a crystal that makes them useful in oscillators?

2. What determines the output frequency of a crystal oscillator?

For the next 5 questions refer to the diagram at right.

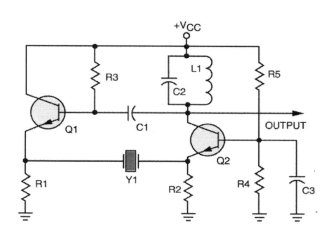

3. What configurations are the two amplifiers in this circuit?

4. What provides the regenerative feedback coupling to the base of Q1 to provide forward bias?

5. What is the purpose of the tank circuit C2 and L1?

6. What is the entire regenerative feedback loop for this circuit?

7. How do you change the output frequency of this device?

Worksheet 39
Chapter 3, Section 9

Filters

1. What is the purpose of an electronic filter?

2. What are the three circuit configurations of a filter?

3. What electrical components make up the construction of an electronic filter?

4. What are the two parts of a filter and which develops the output signal?

   Identify each of the diagrams and draw the output frequency response curve.

5. Diagram 1

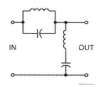

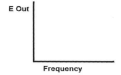

6. Diagram 2

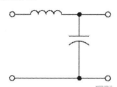

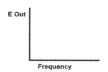

7. Diagram 3

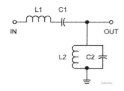

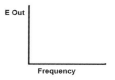

8. Diagram 4

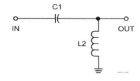

Worksheet 40
Chapter 3, Section 10

Operational Amplifiers

1. What are the two functions that an Op Amp can perform?

2. What are the three characteristics of an Op Amp?

3. When a portion of the signal of the output is fed back into the input is an example of what type of feedback?

4. What happens to the signal when de-generative feedback is applied?

Worksheet 41
Chapter 3, Section 10

Wave Generation Circuits

1. What two electrical components would generate a sawtooth waveform?

2. What are the three basic configurations of multivibrator circuits?

3. For a one shot multivibrator what determines the maximum length of the square wave?

4. For the output of the multivibrator circuit, how is the PRF determined?

5. What are the two outputs called in an SR Flip Flop?

6. What makes an astable multivibrator operate as an oscillator?

7. How many transistors can conduct at a time in a multivibrator circuit?

For the next 4 questions refer to the multivibrator drawing below.

8. Which two resistors determine the charge time of the capacitors C3 and C4?

9. Which resistor is designed to adjust the frequency of the oscillator?

10. What type of waveform is produced by an Astable Multivibrator circuit?

11. What is the discharge path for capacitor C3?

12. In the astable multivibrator, moving the arm of R6 to the right will:

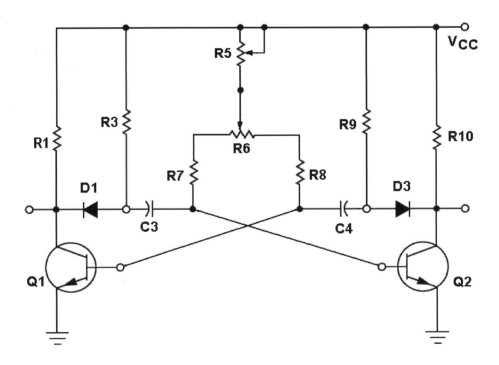

Worksheet 42
Chapter 4, Section 1

Batteries

1. What are the two classifications of batteries?

2. Which of category of battery cannot be recharged?

3. For a wet cell battery, what are the two elements that make up the electrodes?

4. What is an atom called that is either positively or negatively charged?

5. What is the solution called that allows those electrons to flow?

6. How much voltage does a typical single dry cell battery produce?

7. What happens to a lead acid battery when the unit is left in a discharge state for a long period of time?

8. What are the two main elements in the construction of a Ni-Cad battery?

9. What is the benefit that the Ni-Cad battery has over it's lead acid counterpart when it compares to the performance of voltage?

10. What negative aspects do Ni-Cads have that a technician needs to be aware of when charging the cell?

11. With no load applied to the battery, what is the reading called?

12. With a OCV of 14.2Vdc and a CCV of 11.6Vdc and a load of 85Amps, what is the series equivalent resistance of the battery?

13. What are the two types of lead acid batteries that can be used in aviation?

14. When individual battery cells are connected in series what happens to the current and the voltage of the combined cells?

Worksheet 43
Chapter 4, Section 1

Battery Maintenance

1. For a charged lead acid battery, what is the ratio of water to acid?

2. For a lead acid battery what is added to the lead material and why?

3. In an aviation battery, how are vents caps different than automotive units?

4. What causes plate shorting in a lead acid battery as it ages?

5. When disconnecting a battery from an aircraft, which cable is disconnected first?

6. For a lead acid battery what is the tool used to indicate the state of charge of the electrolyte?

7. What are the two types of battery chargers available to technicians?

8. Which one of the chargers in the previous question should never be connected to an aircraft?

Worksheet 44
Chapter 4, Section 2

Switches

1. What are the two parts of mechanical switch?

2. What is a basic toggle switch in aircraft installations?

3. What is a multi-throw switch?

4. A momentary on switch is used for what in an aircraft radio installation?

5. Refer to the diagrams and identify the various switch types.

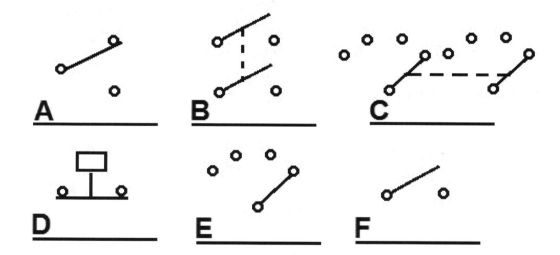

A _____   B _____   C _____

D _____   E _____   F _____

Worksheet 45
Chapter 4, Section 2

Relays

1. What is the use of an electrical relay in an aircraft?

2. What is the only moving part of a relay?

3. What pulls the armature onto the core?

4. What are the devices in the relay that make the electrical connections?

5. What might cause a relay not to actuate (or move inside) when a current is applied?

6. What type of relay is built very strongly, has a core that is pulled into the electromagnet, and is designed to handle high current loads?

7. What is the use of an overload relay?

8. What are the three basic mechanical parts of a relay that could malfunction?

9. When performing a check of a coil with a multimeter, what would a reading of infinity indicate?

10. Refer to the diagram below and give the multimeter reading in volts between the test point and ground.

     a. Pin 7 _____
     b. Pin 5 _____
     c. Pin 8 _____
     d. Pin 2 _____
     e. Pin 3 _____
     f. Pin 1 _____

Worksheet 46
Chapter 4, Section 2

Sensors

1. Under what electrical principle do proximity sensors work?

2. For a proximity sensor, what does putting a steel target next to it do?

3. In a fuel quantity indicating system for large aircraft, what small electrical component are the fuel probes constructed like?

4. How are fuel probes wired in the tank that allow them to average the fuel level inside throughout the flight?

5. What is the physical property of a bimetallic junction that is used in devices such as temperature probes?

6. What is produced when you bond alumel and chromel together and apply heat?

7. What is an example of a position sensor in an aircraft?

8. What can be a problem with using a simple variable resistor for in a fuel, or some other calibrated indicating system?

9. What is the circuit called that can give accurate variable resistance readings no matter the system voltage?

Worksheet 47
Chapter 4, Section 3

Number Systems Conversions

For each number please convert the decimal number to Binary, Octal and Hexadecimal.

1. 25_{10}
   Binary_____

   Octal_____

   Hexadecimal_____

2. 102_{10}
   Binary_____

   Octal_____

   Hexadecimal_____

3. 86_{10}
   Binary_____

   Octal_____

   Hexadecimal_____

4. 135_{10}
   Binary_____

   Octal_____

   Hexadecimal_____

5. 281_{10}
   Binary_____

   Octal_____

   Hexadecimal_____

6. 44_{10}
   Binary_____

   Octal_____

   Hexadecimal_____

7. 1001_{10}
   Binary_____

   Octal_____

   Hexadecimal_____

8. 222_{10}
   Binary_____

   Octal_____

   Hexadecimal_____

Worksheet 48
Chapter 4, Section 3

Binary Addition/Subtraction

Add

1. 110001
   +11001

4. 11000
   +111

2. 100100
   +110100

5. 10101
   +1111

3. 100100
   + 111111

6. 10011
   +1010

Subtract.

7. 10001
   -110

10. 10001
    - 110

8. 111001
   -100

11. 100111
    - 1000

9. 1001
   - 11

12. 11001
    - 110

Worksheet 49
Chapter 4, Section 3

Binary Multiplication/Division

Multiply   Divide

1.   100010
         x   10

                                        5.   10 ⟌ 1100

2.   101010
         x 101

                                        6.   101 ⟌ 1111

3.   111001
         x 1001

                                        7.   111 ⟌ 1001101

4.   101000
         x 1010

Worksheet 50
Chapter 4, Section 4

Logic Gates

1. What are the two states that describe the outputs/inputs of a logic circuit?

2. What is the purpose of a logic gate in electrical diagrams?

3. What is "Logic Function" as it refers to gate operation?

4. What is used to help describe all of the possible outcomes to a given input of a logic gate?

5. What logic device is it, that all inputs must be high before a high can be given at the output?

6. What logic device is used as a single signal in and single output device designed to inverse the output to the input signal?

7. What is added to a AND Gate that makes it a NAND Gate?

8. What is used to plot the actions of various numbers and types gates over time?

9. What is the plot that cycles on and off in a predictable manner called on a chart?

Worksheet 51
Chapter 4, Section 4

Complete Logic Truth Tables and Identify the Gate

Logic Truth Tables

A —o|>— Output

A	Output
0	
1	

1. _____

A —⊐&⊃— Output
B

A	B	Output
0	0	
0	1	
1	0	
1	1	

2. _____

A —⊐≥1⊃— Output
B

A	B	Output
0	0	
0	1	
1	0	
1	1	

3. _____

A —⊐)o— Output
B

A	B	Output
0	0	
0	1	
1	0	
1	1	

4. _____

A —⊐&o— Output
B

A	B	Output
0	0	
0	1	
1	0	
1	1	

5. _____

A —⊐)o— Output
B

A	B	Output
0	0	
0	1	
1	0	
1	1	

6. _____

A —⊐)⊃— Output
B

A	B	Output
0	0	
0	1	
1	0	
1	1	

7. _____

A —o⊐&⊃— Output
B —o

A	B	Output
0	0	
0	1	
1	0	
1	1	

8. _____

A —o⊐)⊃— Output
B —o

A	B	Output
0	0	
0	1	
1	0	
1	1	

9. _____

Worksheet 52
Chapter 4, Section 4

Flip Flops and Counters

1. What is the primary purpose of a Flip Flop in electrical circuits?

Refer to the diagram at right and answer the following.

2. What type of flip flop is this?

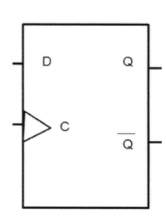

3. What are the three inputs of this device?

4. When a clock trigger is sent to this device, when does this device change its state?

5. What is the output when both S and R are 1 or high?

Refer to the diagram at right for the next 4 questions

6. What type of Flip Flop is this?

7. What sets the output Q to 0?

8. What does $\overline{Q}$ mean?

Using the diagrams below and at right complete the truth table

9. Solve

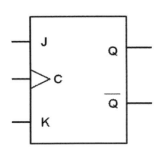

J	K	C	Q	Q̄	Operation
0	0				
0	1				
1	0				
1	1				

10. Complete the plot of the graph using the truth table you completed above graph the Q output graph. Assume that Q is at 1 to start.

Truth Table

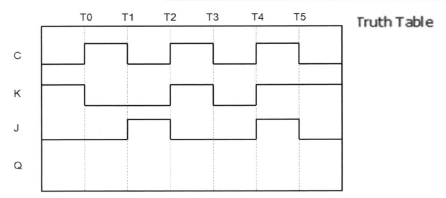

11. What is the diagram at right?

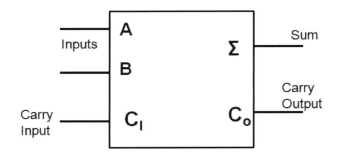

12. What is the diagram at right?

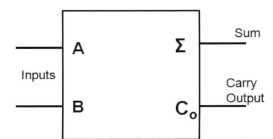

13. In the space below draw the logic diagram for a full adder.

Worksheet 53
Chapter 5, Section 1

Aircraft Wiring

1. What US standards must aircraft wire meet to be eligible for installation in aircraft?

2. What are the general physical characteristics of aircraft wire that make it different from automotive or industrial wire?

3. What are the general forms or types of aircraft wire?

4. Name two of the best conductive materials and what in their construction makes them the best?

5. What are the two best insulating materials and what is the unique atomic make up of these materials that drive their unique characteristics.

6. Identify the makeup and construction of the most common aircraft wire including the wire coatings and temperature ratings.

7. Identify the characteristics of an insulator that inhibits the flow of electrons.

8. Identify the causes of radio frequency interference (RFI) and how it is dealt with in aircraft construction?

9. What is the minimum size of aluminum wire that can be used in aircraft and what consideration must be made for aluminum wire connections?

10. What is the industry standard used to specify wire diameters and what is the incremental size number that will either double of halve the size of the wire?

11. What is the purpose of the wire usage chart and where is the chart available for a technician to refer to (an FAA document)?

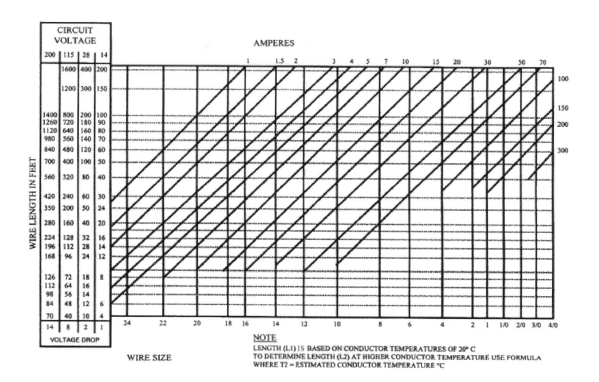

CIRCUIT VOLTAGE

AMPERES

WIRE LENGTH IN FEET

VOLTAGE DROP

WIRE SIZE

Using the wire usage chart and following the instructions in the FAA document, select the system voltage, the wire run distance, the component amperage draw and determine the size of the wire necessary to meet the minimum FAA requirements.

12. Using the chart find: the minimum wire size needed for a voltage of 28VDC, for a length of 40 feet, with a load of 5 amps of a wire in a conduit.

13. Using the chart find: the minimum wire size needed for a voltage of 115 VAC, for a length of 96 feet, with a load of 30 amps of a wire in free air.

14. Using the chart find: the minimum wire size needed for a voltage of 14VDC, for a length of 10 feet, with a load of 10 amps of a wire in free air.

Worksheet 54

Chapter 5, Section 2

Blueprints and Technical Drawings

1. What are the 3 types of basic technical drawings used in the aircraft industry? Describe aircraft components and structure?

2. There are 13 specific types of lines used in typical aircraft drawings. If you wanted to find out what each line represents where could you go for the information?

3. What are the purpose section lines that are placed in a typical drawing?

4. How are three view drawings used by technicians?

5. What was the purpose of using the blueprint processes in the past?

6. Do detail drawings have enough detail to be able to duplicate every aspect of the part?

7. What is the purpose of assembly drawings in maintenance manuals?

8. What is the purpose of installation drawings and what important information do they provide?

9. When would the sectional drawing be used?

10. Exploded view drawings typically are the same drawings and are used in what two documents?

Worksheet 55

Chapter 5, Section 3

Reading Aircraft Diagrams

1. What can a block diagram describe to the technician?

2. Can a block diagram show more than just electrical inputs?

3. Name a primary purpose of a flow chart used in aircraft maintenance manuals.

4. What is the main difference between a flow chart and a logic diagram?

5. What is the primary purpose of a pictorial diagram?

6. Are system schematics used for any other purpose than to describe electronic systems?

7. Do electrical schematics show the same level of detail throughout the schematic?

8. In what section would you find the descriptions of the symbols in the wiring diagram manual?

9. What is the symbol to indicate that wires are twisted in ATA drawings?

10. What is the wire identification pattern used in ATA wiring diagram manuals?

11. What are the primary power types that can be used for large transport aircraft?

12. What is the aircraft electrical section called that is receiving power from the generators?

13. When it comes to electrical conversion, what is the difference between a GA and a transport category aircraft?

Worksheet 56

Chapter 5, Section 2

Electrical to Mechanical Schematic Reading

For the questions in this section, refer to the drawing found in the NCATT AET page 233.

1. Using electrical/mechanical schematic what position is the relay for the landing light when the light is retracted?

2. What is used to determine the direction of the motor?

3. Describe all of the NO contacts when the light is retracted?

4. What is the switch type for the cockpit control?

5. When the switch is set to the extend position what component/s become energized right away?

6. What two conditions must be met before the light bulb will illuminate?

7. How do you know that the light will move with the motor in this drawing?

8. Refer to the magnetic motor brake, where does the voltage come from to release it?

9. What is the electrical configuration of this motor?

Simple troubleshooting

10. When the switch is turned on and nothing happens. You can hear the relay actuate, you measure voltage coming out of the relay. What is the next component in the circuit that should have voltage?

11. You actuate the switch and the motor cycles fully down but the light never turns on. What is the first thing to test before dismantling the components?

12. When you actuate the switch the motor begins to drive and the light illuminates. When the light becomes fully extended the motor is slowed down briefly and then the circuit breaker opens. What would cause the breaker to open?

13. When the pilot attempts to retract the light the lamp goes out but the motor does not move. What would cause the light to out but not allow the motor to retract?

Worksheet 57

Chapter 6, Section 1

Aircraft Workplace Safety

1. What are the 2 main types of physical injuries attributed to electricity?

2. What is the cause of an electrical burn to the human body?

3. The severity of a shock to the human body depends on what 3 conditions?

4. What is the most common shock related injury that occurs in the workplace?

5. What problem would develop if a circuit breaker is too large for the system?

6. What is the most frequently violated OSHA regulation that relates to wiring?

7. How does a Ground Fault Interrupter (GFI) sense a ground condition?

8. With a GFI installed in a circuit, what would be the most evident condition that a problem exists if no power is at the sockets?

9. What should technicians do in the cockpit to protect themselves from injury prior to working on an aircraft system away from the cockpit?

Worksheet 58

Chapter 6, Section 1

Personal Protection Equipment/ESDS

1. Personal Protective Equipment (PPE) shoes protect the technician from impacts. What else should the shoes protect the technician from?

2. What should be the priority as it comes to PPE before working on electrical equipment?

3. What are the two primary protections that hard hats provide?

4. Define electrostatic discharge (ESD)?

5. How does ESD concern avionics technicians?

6. How many volts does an ESD discharge need to be to damage electronic equipment?

7. What is upset damage caused by an ESD?

8. What is latent damage caused by an ESD and would there be an indication of damage?

9. What is catastrophic failure definition that is caused by an ESD?

10. What kind of personal grounding is necessary to protect from an ESD?

11. What is a dissipative work surface?

12. What is the purpose of an MSDS document?

13. What makes a compound a HAZMAT that requires special handling?

14. Where should a copy of a MSDS document be kept?

15. In what part of the document should a technician know before ever working with a HAZMAT?

Worksheet 59
Chapter 7, Section 1

Aerodynamics and Balance

1. What did the Wright brothers discover during flight testing of their 1902 glider that made stable flight possible?

2. What do you call the movement about the lateral axis of an aircraft?

3. What kind of a control surface did the Wright brothers use to control movement about the lateral axis and where was it mounted on the aircraft?

4. Roll is the movement around the longitudinal axis. What did the Wright brothers use to affect the roll movement in their aircraft?

5. What control surface is used to control yaw of the aircraft?

6. *Adverse yaw* is caused by which control surface deflection?

7. What must the pilot do to overcome adverse yaw?

Worksheet 60

Chapter 7, Section 1

Forces Acting on an Aircraft

1. What are the 4 forces acting on an aircraft in stable flight?

2. What causes the lower pressure on the top of a wing compared to the bottom of the wing for an aircraft in flight?

3. Describe the upper camber of a wing?

4. What determines the angle of attack of a wing in flight?

5. If you increase the angle of attack of the wing within its normal operating parameters, what is the effect on the aircraft performance?

6. If you increase the angle of attack beyond the normal flight envelope of the aircraft, what will happen?

7. What is the typical source of thrust in GA aircraft?

8. What are the 2 types of drag that occurred during normal operation of an aircraft?

9. Which type of drag is inversely proportional to airspeed?

10. Define wing loading.

11. What causes wing tip vortices?

12. What is added to a wing to minimizing the effect of wing tip vortices?

Worksheet 61

Chapter 7, Section 1

Flight Controls

1. Where are the ailerons located on an aircraft and how do the two surfaces relate to each other?

2. What is the section called that contains the flight crew and passengers and has the wings and empennage attached to it?

3. What are the primary purpose of the wings?

4. What parts of an aircraft are included as the empennage?

5. What parts of the empennage actually move to directly control the aircraft in flight?

6. Where are the flaps installed on an aircraft?

7. What functions do flaps provide for the performance of the aircraft?

8. What are the two types of landing gear installed on aircraft?

9. What purpose does the rudder have in controlling the aircraft in flight?

10. What does the elevator do to control the aircraft in flight?

Worksheet 62

Chapter 7, Section 1

Primary and Secondary Flight Controls

1. What are the primary flight controls of an aircraft?

2. What are the lift augmenting devices that are attached to wings?

3. What are the purposes of spoilers?

4. As flaps extend out past the trailing edge of the wings, what effects does it have on the aerodynamics?

5. How do flaps help an aircraft in the landing phase?

6. What are the purposes of the slots in the flaps?

7. What does the addition of leading and trailing edge devices do to the wing when extended?

8. For an air carrier leading edge device, what best describes the *Kruger* flaps?

9. What are the two classifications of spoilers used on large air carrier aircraft?

Worksheet 63
Chapter 7, Section 1

Aircraft Trim Systems

1. What is the primary purpose of the aircraft trim system?

2. How does a trim tab affect the flight control that it is attached to?

3. If an elevator trim tap is moved up into the airflow, how does it affect the elevator and therefore the aircraft pitch?

4. For a simple aircraft trim system, what does a bungee cord do for the flight controls?

5. How can trim systems be actuated in a typical aircraft?

6. In an air carrier aircraft elevator trim system, what large surface is moved when the trim system is actuated?

7. To prevent inadvertent stabilizer trim actuation, what do air carrier aircraft have as part of the design to prevent this?

Worksheet 64

Chapter 7, Section 1

Aircraft Stability

1. What are the three types of stability that are involved in aircraft operations?

2. When aircraft pitch is upset and the nose continues in the direction of the upset in an ever increasing rate, what type of stability does this aircraft have?

3. For the average aircraft, what type of stability is desired and why?

4. For yaw stability what has to be done to the aircraft design to allow the aircraft to return to straight flight?

5. Lateral stability is about what axis?

6. What is built into aircraft wings to build automatic lateral stability?

7. What is built into aircraft for longitudinal stability?

8. How does increasing airspeed in an aircraft affect the aerodynamics of the aircraft?

9. What in a piston engine aircraft causes left turning tendencies?

Worksheet 65

Chapter 7, Section 1

Aircraft Construction

1. What are aircraft designers always trying to balance when designing and constructing new aircraft?

2. What is classified as primary structure for aircraft?

3. What type of wing construction is most associated with bridges?

4. What type of fuselage structure is totally internally braced?

5. For the aircraft type listed above, what is it called when a structure needs to add a single brace or strut?

6. In a monocoque fuselage, what is the structure called that runs from front to back of the aircraft?

7. What is added to a fuselage to reinforce sections such as doorways and pressure sections?

8. What part of a wing has the most strength and is bolted to the fuselage?

9. What structural feature installed in wings shape the airfoil?

Worksheet 66
Chapter 7, Section 1
Aircraft Weight and Balance

1. Why is the concept of balance so important to aircraft loading?

2. Compared to a fulcrum, what is the same point on an aircraft?

3. What are the three items that are being balanced in level flight?

4. What is the datum of an aircraft and what is the unit of measure in US certificated aircraft?

5. What is the significance of the moment number?

6. How is the total moment calculated?

7. How is the center of gravity calculated?

8. What is the measure for the location of the datum from the center of gravity?

9. When the whole aircraft needs to have the center of gravity determined and taking the measure of each individual component is not practical, how could a mechanic determine a new CG?

10. What aircraft document must be updated in addition to the aircraft maintenance records when making changes to the aircraft weight and balance?

11. What is defined as the CG range for an aircraft?

12. What is the danger of loading an aircraft in the most aft CG location?

13. Using the original aircraft weight and balance information, determine a new empty center of gravity when you install a new electric trim motor in the back of the aircraft. The acceptable range is 35 to 47 inches.

	Weight	CG	Total Moment
Empty Weight	1,683	39.7	66,815

Installation of new motor: location from Datum - 117.00 inches
Weight of new motor - 5.4 lbs

Worksheet 67
Chapter 7, Section 2

Aircraft Corrosion

1. What two elements can cause corrosion on metal surfaces?

2. What are electrically conductive solutions that cause corrosion in aircraft structure?

3. How many types of major classifications of corrosion that can damage aircraft structure?

4. What material in metal creates the grains that cause corrosion to develop deep inside the sub straight?

5. What is it that is flowing on a surface of metals when an electrolyte is present that facilitates corrosion?

6. What property of metal creates situations that make it corrode more readily?

7. What agents cause the most corrosion on metals?

8. What are alkalies and what causes them?

9. What is general surface corrosion called, and how is it recognized?

10. When a dull and gray powdery surface is cleaned away and surfaces of tiny holes are revealed, what type of damage is present?

11. In what surfaces are crevice or concentration cell corrosion found?

12. What type of corrosion is caused when two dissimilar metals are immersed in an electrolytic solution?

13. What type of corrosion can be hidden deep in metals in which structural failure can be the first indication of a problem?

14. What is necessary to prevent corrosion in aircraft metal surfaces?

Worksheet 68
Chapter 7, Section 3

Instructions for Continued Airworthiness

1. What is issued to all aircraft that are manufactured to specific FAA standards?

2. What is a Type Design as it pertains to aircraft?

3. What is the Federal Air Regulation that describes the minimum standard for how aircraft less than 12000 lbs are constructed and approved for certification in the U.S.?

4. What are required to be developed that meet the requirements for the instructions for continued airworthiness?

5. For large air carrier aircraft what system is used to organize all of the many subject areas that involved in the maintenance and repair of the aircraft?

6. What major elements are included in a structural repair manual?

7. When selecting a wiring diagram for a large air carrier aircraft, what does the technician need to find out when selecting the proper diagram?

8. What FAR covers the required elements that a mechanic needs to comply with after performing maintenance?

9. When a name of a person is required in the record and the person works for a FAR 145 repair station, what number is signed on the record?

10. When work is being performed by un-certificated personnel, whose name is entered into the aircraft record?

11. When FAR 43.9 requires approved data, who is that approved by?

12. What is issued by the FAA when a safety of flight issue exists?

13. What is the difference between a service bulletin and an airworthiness directive?

14. When recording a major alteration or repair, what document is required to be completed and forwarded to the FAA?

15. What can be used for acceptable data in block 8 on a FAA Form 337?

16. When a repair or alteration is required and the technician wants to use other acceptable data from another aircraft for installation in the one you are working on, what application process can be used?

Worksheet 69
Chapter 7, Section 4

Basic Electrical Troubleshooting

1. What is the major troubleshooting technique that needs to be learned before working on an aircraft system?

2. To prepare the system for troubleshooting what is the first step that a technician needs to ensure?

3. If the system will not turn on with the normal switches, what do you look at next?

4. For some modern aircraft systems, what could you do to verify if the system/box is operating basically well?

5. What simple test equipment is needed to be able to test individual wires in an aircraft?

6. What are the four basic tests that can be performed by a multimeter?

7. What semiconductor device can also be tested with most modern multimeters?

8. When using the ammeter function of a multimeter, how would you connect the leads to the circuit?

9. What is an ammeter shunt?

10. When placing multimeter leads in a circuit, what is being measured in the voltmeter?

11. When using a multimeter to check a fuse in a circuit, what is read on the meter when the leads are connected as shown?

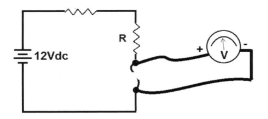

12. When measuring a device in a circuit using an Ohmmeter, how should you connect the meter?

Worksheet 70
Chapter 7, Section 4

Using an Oscilloscope

1. What is the primary purpose of an oscilloscope?

2. Describe the two axis that can be plotted onto the graph of an oscilloscope?

3. For a typical oscilloscope what are the divisions of the screen?

4. What is the white line on the display called?

5. For the diagram at right what is the type of signal?

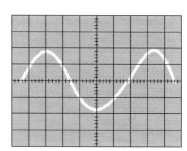

6. What is a non-periodically or infrequently occurring signal that could be displayed on an oscilloscope?

7. To move a trace up and down on the display, what control needs to be adjusted?

8. Refer to the trace plot at right, how would you make the wave more visible in the screen?

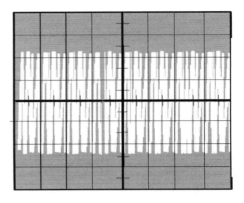

9. What device is used to produce a calibrated signal that can be compared to the signal under test?

10. What is meant when a technician uses an O-scope to probe a circuit board?

Worksheet 71
Chapter 7, Section 4

Testing Basic Components

1. What are the two ways that resistors can fail in a circuit?

2. How can a resistor be tested when it is in a circuit?

3. What tester is used to measure a resistor before that resistor is installed in a circuit?

4. When testing a diode with a multimeter, how are the leads connected to the diode?

5. How can you use a multimeter to test a capacitor?

6. How does a condenser tester work on a capacitor?

7. When measuring an inductor using a multimeter, what are you measuring?

8. How a transformer is tested using a multimeter?

9. Refer to the diagram at right and give the expected readings on an Ohmmeter.

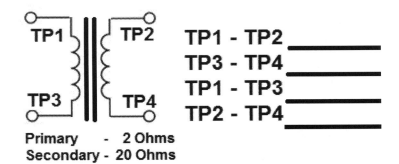

Primary   - 2 Ohms
Secondary - 20 Ohms

TP1 - TP2 _____
TP3 - TP4 _____
TP1 - TP3 _____
TP2 - TP4 _____

10. Using the diagram above, what does a reading of 0.02Ohms between TP3 and TP4 indicate?

11. Using the diagram above, what does a reading of infinity between TP2 and TP4 indicate?

12. When measuring a relay what are the circuits that need to be tested?

13. Refer to the diagram at right and identify the contacts.

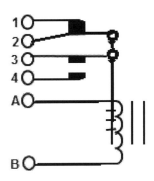

1 and 2 _____

3 and 4 _____

A and B _____

14. An open between A and B is an indication of what?

15. When you place an Ohmmeter on pin 1 and 2 and read 230KΩ, what could this be an indication of?

Worksheet 72
Chapter 7, Section 4

Measuring Voltage in a Circuit

Using the diagram provided determine the voltage that should be read on a volt meter when always placing the leads as indicated.

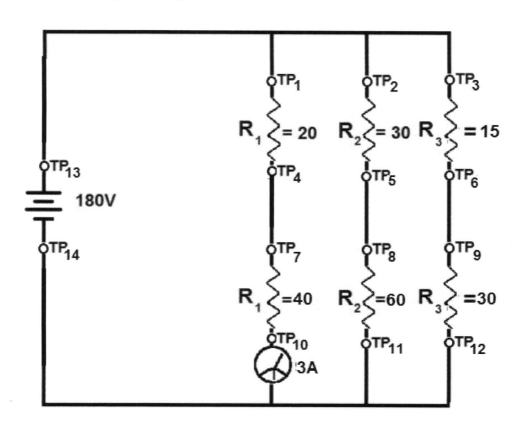

1. TP1 to TP10 _____

2. TP2 to TP5 _____

3. TP3 to TP14 _____

4. TP4 to TP7 _____

5. TP1 to TP12 _____

6. TP7 to TP14 _____

7. TP5 to TP11 _____

8. TP9 to TP10 _____

9. TP13 to TP12 _____

Worksheet 73
Chapter 7, Section 5

Tools and Safety Devices

1. What is the difference between a hammer and a mallet?

2. What is the physical difference between a Phillips and a Reed &Prince tip screwdriver?

3. How are Phillips screwdrivers sized?

4. How does a high torque bit differ from a standard straight slot?

5. What is used that can quickly turn screw fasteners?

6. What are the two types of construction of aircraft sockets?

7. What is the best style of socket used when removing a nut off of a long bolt?

8. What is a wrench called that completely surrounds a fasteners head?

9. Fixed joint pliers are named for what?

10. When using a movable jaw tool to remove a fitting, which jaw is placed in the pulling direction?

Worksheet 74
Chapter 7, Section 5

Wire Strippers and Connectors

1. When stripping the wire off of aircraft type wire, what should the tool not do to the conductor?

2. What are some problems with using an automotive type stripper on aircraft wiring?

3. What makes a stripper an automatic one used for aircraft wiring?

4. What makes a wire stripper suitable for aircraft use?

5. When using aircraft style crimps, why is using automotive style crimpers not a good idea?

6. When you look at a crimp that was done using a proper crimper, what is most noticeable about the crimps?

7. What is the color code for an AWG 22 to 16 wire?

8. What can be adjusted for a Red/Blue crimping tool?

9. What is a MOLEX style connector?

10. There are two crimps being made by an MOLEX connector, what is the purpose of each individual crimp?

11. What are the three sections of a MOLEX connector?

12. For MOLEX type connections, where are they commonly used in general aviation aircraft?

13. What do MOLEX connectors have that prevents wrong type radios from being inserted into a rack?

14. What makes a Cannon style plug much different than traditional MOLEX connectors?

15. What are the two types of conductors that are used in Cannon style connectors?

16. Cannon plugs are mated from what to what?

17. For Cannon plug numbering of the contacts, what letters are not used?

18. What is used to number the various types of contacts?

19. What crimp characteristics are required for Cannon plug contacts?

20. For a red and white cannon plug tool, which end is used for insertion?

Worksheet 75
Chapter 7, Section 5

Safety Devices

1. Why is there a need to safety wire turnbuckles, nuts or bolts?

2. What type of safety wire should be used to secure emergency items such as fire extinguishers, door handles or switch guards that might be needed in an emergency?

3. What is the most common method of safety wiring used that is for widely spaced nuts and bolts?

4. What method can be used when safeting closely spaced nuts, screws or bolts?

5. What minimum size of safety wire should be used on parts that have a hole diameter larger than 0.045 inch?

6. Refer to the diagram at right and draw the wire pattern.

7. Refer the bolts at right and draw how you would safety these three bolts?

8. What is required for the use of a cotter pin?

9. What should you do when installing a cotter pin to prevent injury to other technicians?

10. When inserting a cotter pin into a bolt, how should the cotter pin tangs be bent?

Worksheet Answers

Worksheet 1

Chapter 1, Section 1 DC Terms

1 –The Electrons located in the outer orbits of atoms are associated with current flow.

2 – Whether or not there contains free electrons in the orbits of the atoms

3 – Static electricity is a difference of electrical charge between two non-conductive surfaces.

4 – Amperes is the amount of current flowing past a particular point in the circuit

5 – A basic unit of electrical quantity equal to 6.28 X 10^{18} or 6.28 billion-billion electrons.

6 – Electron Motive Force (EMF) or Volts.

7 – To determine the current in a circuit, the voltage is divided by the resistance. $I = \dfrac{E}{R}$

8 – A capacitor

9 – This describes the flow of current in a conductor when passed through magnetic lines of flux. The thumb represents the motion of the conductor, the index finger represents the line of flux of the magnetic field and the middle finger is the resultant current flow.

10 – The ease of which the lines of flux follow the material is determined by the permeability of the material that the lines of flux are directed to flow through.

11 - To save wires all return paths to the negative electrical potential by using an earth or chassis ground.

12 – A larger amount of resistance will slow the rate of current flow.

13 – Ohms law is where the electrical pressure of 1 volt is equal to the flow of 1 amp of current times the resistance of 1 ohm.

14 – One watt of energy is equal to 1/746th of a horsepower

15 – The flow of current is common across all resistance loads around the circuit.

16- In a parallel circuit the voltage is equal across the branches while current will be cumulative of each branch.

17 – Thumb = direction of motion of conductor, index finger the direction of the magnetic field and the middle finger = the resultant current flow.

18 – Static electricity has no useful purpose in aviation.

19- Only materials that have high permeability will pass lines of magnetic flux,

20 – The basic unit of measure for a capacitor is a Farad.

21 – A battery that is called primary cannot be recharged while a secondary can be.

Worksheet 2

Chapter 1, Section 2

1. Symbol for a resistor.
2. By a number reference to the manufacture, by a set of color bands and by direct measurement.

3. A rheostat, potentiometer and a tapped resistor

4. A resistor is design to impede the flow of current in a circuit in two ways, by slowing the overall current in a series circuit and by providing biasing for voltage in parallel branches.

5. This is the multiplier of the number represented by the first two numbers while the third color is the multipler by 10 the first two numbers.

6. Ohms law cannot apply to resistors that are changed by variations in heat or light.

7. This is the percentage of resistance value that any resistor can maintain through a range of current. For example a 1000 ohms resistor with a Silver band can be expected to maintain its value $\pm$ 100 ohms or 10%.

Resistor Color Codes

8. $5\Omega \pm 5\%$

9. $62K\Omega$ or $62,000\Omega \pm 10\%$

10. $11\Omega \pm 20\%$

11. $900,000\Omega \pm 10\%$

12. The ability for a resistor to withstand more or less wattage based on the physical size of the diameter of the resistor.

Worksheet 3
Chapter 1 Section 3
1. Voltage (E) is the total product of current (I) and Resistance (R) E=IXR

2. Current (I) is the total of the division between Voltage (E) divided by Resistance (Ω). I = E/R

3. Resistance (Ω) is the total of the division of voltage (E) by current (A) R = E/I

4. E = 2a X 5Ω E = 10V

5. I = 12/6 I = 2a

6. R = 120/60 R = 2A

7. Power, measured in Watts (P) is the product of Voltage (E) and Current (I). P = I X E

8. P = 60a X 110V P = 6600Watts or P = 6.6 Kilowatts

Worksheet 4
Chapter 1, Section 4
1. A reference point is an arbitrary location on a circuit where a measurement can be compared to.

2. The total voltage of this circuit is the sum of all of the voltage drops of each resistor.

3. The current total in the circuit is equal across each resistor equally.

4. 50 Volts

5. 0 Volts

6. 75 Volts

7. 25 Volts

Worksheet 5
Chapter 1, Section 5
1. That the total resistance in a series circuit is the sum of all of the resistors. $R^T = R_1 + R_2 + R_3$

2. The Total Current in a series circuit is equal across all of the resistors equally $I^T = I_{R1} = I_{R2} = I_{R3}$

3. The total voltage of a series is equal to the sum of the voltage drops of each resistor. $E^T = E_{R1} + E_{R2} + E_{R3}$

4. $R^T = 30 + 10 + 15$ $R^T = 55\Omega$

5. $I^T = 135/45$ $I^T = 2.45a$

6. $E_{R2} = 10 \times 3$ $E_{R2} = 24.5V$

7. $R^T = 4K + 6K + 10K$ $R^T = 20K$ $ET = 20K \times 5mA$ $ET = 100Volts$

8. $ER3 = 10K \times 5mA$ $ER3 = 30V$

Worksheet 6
Chapter 1, Section 5

1. The E_T is equal across the branches of the circuit. $E_T = E_{R1} = E_{R2} = E_{R3}$

2. The IT is the sum of the current in all of the branches. $I_T = I_{R1} + I_{R2} + I_{R3}$

3. The total resistance in a parallel is equal to the sum of the inverse, inversed. $\frac{1}{R} = \frac{1}{R} + \frac{1}{R} + \frac{1}{R}$

---

4. The formula $\frac{1}{R_T} = \frac{1}{10} + \frac{1}{40} + \frac{1}{80}$ Key strokes

$$
\begin{array}{ll}
10 \;\boxed{1/x} & = .1 \\
40 \;\boxed{1/x} & = .025 \\
80 \;\boxed{1/x} & = .0125 \\
\hline
& .1375 \quad \boxed{1/x} = 7.27\,\Omega
\end{array}
$$

---

5. The formula $R_T = \frac{10 \times 10}{10 + 10}$ Key Strokes

$$
\begin{array}{l}
\underline{10}\;\boxed{\times}\;\underline{10}\;\boxed{=}\;\underline{100} \\
\underline{10}\;\boxed{+}\;\underline{10}\;\boxed{=}\;\underline{20}
\end{array}
$$

$100 \;\boxed{\div}\; 20 \;\boxed{=}\; 5\,\Omega$

---

6. The Formula $R_T = \frac{45}{3}$ Key Strokes $45 \;\boxed{\div}\; 3 \;\boxed{=}\; 15\ \Omega$

---

7. Formula for outcome first $I_T = \dfrac{E_T}{R_T}$ Find R_T $\dfrac{10K}{2} = 5K$ $\dfrac{5K}{2} = 2.5K\Omega$

Then use Ohms law for I_T $I_T = \dfrac{9}{2500}$ $I_T = \dfrac{9}{2500} = .0036$

	R_1	R_2	R_3	R_4	R_T
E	9	9	9		9
I	.9mA	.9mA	1.8mA		3.6mA
R	10K	10K	5K		2.5K

Convert I_T = 3.6mA   review chart

---

8. Create chart and fill in the known;

$$\dfrac{1}{20K} + \dfrac{1}{80K} + \dfrac{1}{40K} + \dfrac{1}{80K} = \dfrac{1}{R_T}$$

$.00005 + .0000125 + .000025 + .0000125 = .0001$ $\boxed{1/x}$ $10000\,\Omega$

First determine RT using inverse of the inverse.

	R_1	R_2	R_3	R_4	R_T
E					
I					5mA
R	20K	80K	40K	80K	10K

Use Ohms Law to solve for the E of RT and then because this is a parallel circuit, enter the rest of the voltage.

	R_1	R_2	R_3	R_4	R_T
E	50V	50V	50V	50V	50V
I					5mA
R	20K	80K	40K	80K	10K

E = 10K X 5mA
E = 10000 x .005
E = 50Volts

Then using Ohms Law again solve for current in each branch.

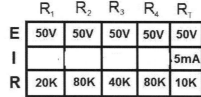

R_1 2.5mA $= \dfrac{50V}{20K}$ $\dfrac{50V}{80K} = .625mA$ R_3

R_2 .625mA $= \dfrac{50V}{80K}$ $\dfrac{50V}{40K} = 1.25mA$ R_4

The final completed chart should look like this> be sure to check your math across the current row.

	R_1	R_2	R_3	R_4	R_T
E	50V	50V	50V	50V	50V
I	2.5mA	.625mA	1.25mA	.625mA	5mA
R	20K	80K	40K	80K	10K

R_T=10KΩ, E_T=50V, E_{R1}=50V, E_{R2}=50V, E_{R3}=50V, I_{R1}=2.5mA, I_{R2}=.625mA, I_{R3}=1.25mA, I_{R4}=.625mA

Worksheet 7

Chapter 1, Section 5

1. Make a chart and fill in the knowns

	R_1	R_2	R_3	R_{EQ}	R_T
E					
I	1				1
R	6	8	8		

There are many ways to solve but we will find RT first then work the problem back out.

$$\frac{8}{2} = R_{EQ} = 4 \qquad\qquad 4+6 = 10\,\Omega = R_T$$

After the total current is determined the applied voltage can be determined, in this case 10V. Now looking at R1 and R2 they share the same current. Using Ohms Laws can determine the voltage drop at each. This total should equal the applied voltage.

	R_1	R_2	R_3	R_{EQ}	R_T
E					10
I	1				1
R	6	8	8	4	10

Now using the rule of parallel branches we know that the voltage across R2 is equal to R3. Then we know at least two of all of the equations and complete the chart to solve the problem.

	R_1	R_2	R_3	R_{EQ}	R_T
E	6	4	4	4	10
I	1	0.5a	0.5a	1	1
R	6	8	8	4	10

R_T= 10Ω, E_T=10V, E_{R1}=6V. E_{R2}=4V, E_{R3}=4V, I_{R1}= 1A. I_{R2}=.5A, I_{R3}=.5A

---

2. Fill in chart. Begin to solve for R_T

$(R_6, R_7) = R_{EQ1}$

$(R_{EQ1}, R_5) = R_{EQ2}$

	R_1	R_2	R_3	R_4	R_5	R_6	R_7	R_{EQ1}	R_{EQ2}	R_{EQ3}	R_T
E											
I											3
R	75	10	15	50	28	33	66				

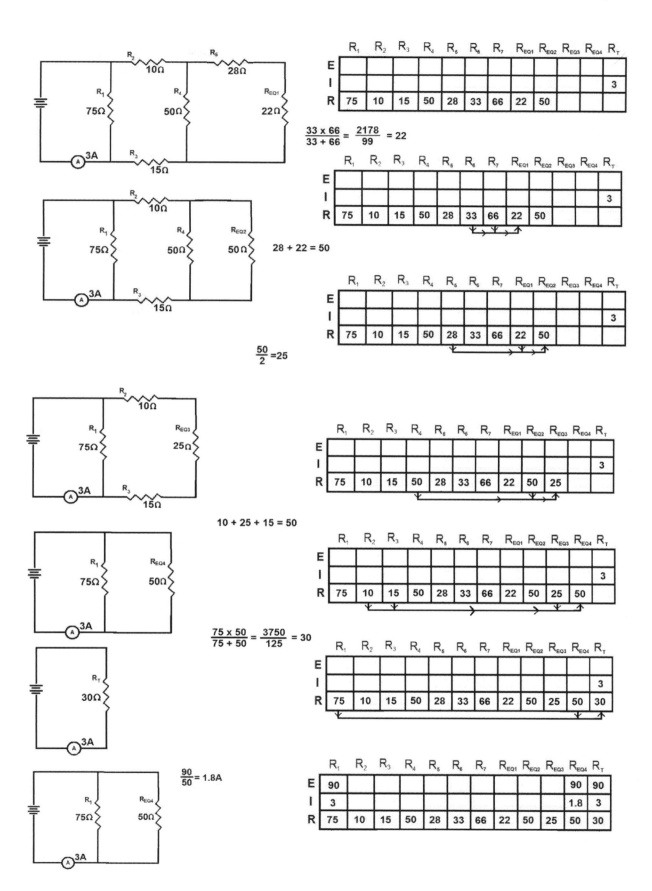

	R_1	R_2	R_3	R_4	R_5	R_6	R_7	R_{EQ1}	R_{EQ2}	R_{EQ3}	R_{EQ4}	R_T
E												
I												3
R	75	10	15	50	28	33	66	22	50			

$$\frac{33 \times 66}{33 + 66} = \frac{2178}{99} = 22$$

	R_1	R_2	R_3	R_4	R_5	R_6	R_7	R_{EQ1}	R_{EQ2}	R_{EQ3}	R_{EQ4}	R_T
E												
I												3
R	75	10	15	50	28	33	66	22	50			

$$28 + 22 = 50$$

	R_1	R_2	R_3	R_4	R_5	R_6	R_7	R_{EQ1}	R_{EQ2}	R_{EQ3}	R_{EQ4}	R_T
E												
I												3
R	75	10	15	50	28	33	66	22	50			

$$\frac{50}{2} = 25$$

	R_1	R_2	R_3	R_4	R_5	R_6	R_7	R_{EQ1}	R_{EQ2}	R_{EQ3}	R_{EQ4}	R_T
E												
I												3
R	75	10	15	50	28	33	66	22	50	25		

$$10 + 25 + 15 = 50$$

	R_1	R_2	R_3	R_4	R_5	R_6	R_7	R_{EQ1}	R_{EQ2}	R_{EQ3}	R_{EQ4}	R_T
E												
I												3
R	75	10	15	50	28	33	66	22	50	25	50	

$$\frac{75 \times 50}{75 + 50} = \frac{3750}{125} = 30$$

	R_1	R_2	R_3	R_4	R_5	R_6	R_7	R_{EQ1}	R_{EQ2}	R_{EQ3}	R_{EQ4}	R_T
E												
I												3
R	75	10	15	50	28	33	66	22	50	25	50	30

$$\frac{90}{50} = 1.8A$$

	R_1	R_2	R_3	R_4	R_5	R_6	R_7	R_{EQ1}	R_{EQ2}	R_{EQ3}	R_{EQ4}	R_T
E	90										90	90
I	3										1.8	3
R	75	10	15	50	28	33	66	22	50	25	50	30

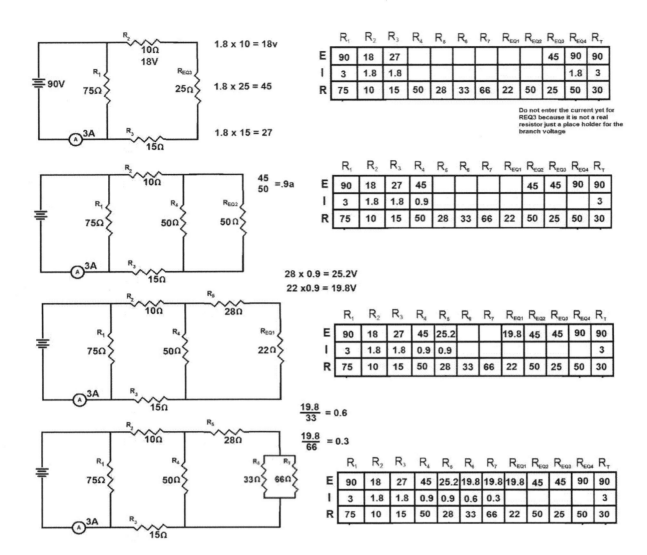

1.8 x 10 = 18v

1.8 x 25 = 45

1.8 x 15 = 27

	R₁	R₂	R₃	R₄	R₅	R₆	R₇	R_EQ1	R_EQ2	R_EQ3	R_EQ4	R_T
E	90	18	27							45	90	90
I	3	1.8	1.8								1.8	3
R	75	10	15	50	28	33	66	22	50	25	50	30

Do not enter the current yet for REQ3 because it is not a real resistor just a place holder for the branch voltage

$\frac{45}{50}$ = .9a

	R₁	R₂	R₃	R₄	R₅	R₆	R₇	R_EQ1	R_EQ2	R_EQ3	R_EQ4	R_T
E	90	18	27	45					45	45	90	90
I	3	1.8	1.8	0.9								3
R	75	10	15	50	28	33	66	22	50	25	50	30

28 x 0.9 = 25.2V
22 x0.9 = 19.8V

	R₁	R₂	R₃	R₄	R₅	R₆	R₇	R_EQ1	R_EQ2	R_EQ3	R_EQ4	R_T
E	90	18	27	45	25.2			19.8	45	45	90	90
I	3	1.8	1.8	0.9	0.9							3
R	75	10	15	50	28	33	66	22	50	25	50	30

$\frac{19.8}{33}$ = 0.6

$\frac{19.8}{66}$ = 0.3

	R₁	R₂	R₃	R₄	R₅	R₆	R₇	R_EQ1	R_EQ2	R_EQ3	R_EQ4	R_T
E	90	18	27	45	25.2	19.8	19.8	19.8	45	45	90	90
I	3	1.8	1.8	0.9	0.9	0.6	0.3					3
R	75	10	15	50	28	33	66	22	50	25	50	30

Worksheet 8

Chapter 2, Section 1

1. AC is the flow of electrons that continuously changes its value in magnitude and periodically reverses electrical polarity.

2. Frequency is the number of times the alternating current starts at 0 then cycles through maximum positive voltage through maximum minimum voltage then back to zero volts.

3. Frequency is defined and the number of cycles of alternating current and is expressed in Hertz (Hz)

4. A Hertz is measured in cycles per second.

5. Impedance is the resistance to current flow in an AC circuit.

6. Reactance is the portion of electrical impedance that is caused by either an inductor or capacitor.

7. Capacitive reactance

8. Current (i) leads Voltage (E) in a capacitance circuit. (ICE)

9. X_C formula $$X_C = \frac{1}{2\pi f C}$$

10. Voltage (E) leads Current (I) in an inductive circuit (ELI)

11. XL formula $$X_L = 2\pi f L$$

12. A sine wave has plots that start at 0 then move thru 90, 180, 270 and then back to zero.

13. When a conductor is passing through 90 and 270 degrees assuming that the conductor starts at zero outside of the magnetic field.

14. The effective value of power for an AC signal is Root Mean Square of the peak voltage.

15. RMS voltage is 0.707% of V_{Peak}

16. Phase angle is the difference between two of more combined signals

17. The power factor is the ratio between the input power compared to the power expended.

18. Reactive power is that power lost in a circuit due to capacitors and inductors.

19. A Wye Wound motor has all phases connected to a common electrical point.

20. A three phase motor is also known as a polyphase winding 120 degrees apart.

21. A rectifier is something that converts AC signals into a DC signal.

22. An inverter will convert DC input into an type of AC output.

23. A voltage drop is measured between a voltage source and load.

24. Kirchhoff's Law for Current

25. A bridge circuit is a device that uses a split circuit and a measurement taken between the two paths.

Worksheet 9
Chapter 2, Section 2

1. An electric generator is a mechanical device that converts mechanical energy into electrical energy.

2. The two types of generators are AC and DC.

3. A commutator is a device when combined with brushes; automatically connects the voltage being produced by the motor out to a load. Because the commutator is connected in a way that produces a DC output.

4. A singe winding generator produces a pulsed DC output where the polarity always is positive.

5. The AC Generator does not require brushes and commutators that produces sparks and sometimes a loss of current due to carbon on the brushes caused by arcing.

6. By rotating a generator more quickly, the output frequency increases.

7. This is a sine wave from a DC generator.

Worksheet 10
Chapter 2, Section 3

1. A cycle is when the voltage and current starts at 0 then through 360 degrees of horizontal travel.

2. Hertz is the unit of measure for frequency.

3. This mathematical formula to determine Hertz is base on the division of a unit of frequency over the period in seconds. (Cycles per seconds)

$$\text{Frequency in Hertz} = \frac{1}{\text{Period in seconds}}$$

4. An oscilloscope is used to graphically plot waveforms.

5. Other waveforms in electronics include square waves, sawtooth waves, and triangle.

6. 123 million cycles per second.

7. AC amplitude is referred to as peak voltage.

8. Peak to Peak is the total amplitude of opposite peaks.

9. True average value of one cycle of AC current or voltage is zero.

10. The equivalent AC power amount to a DC voltage is called the Root Mean Square value of the waveform.

11. RMS is derived by multiplying the peak to peak by .707.

12. Using 12 volts peak the RMS would be 12 x .707= 8.48v RMS

Worksheet 11
Chapter 2, Section 4

1. The values of the resistors are calculated exactly the same for AC as DC circuits.

2. Remember to keep the values alike, if a voltage is peak to peak or RMS, the mathematics must be done in like units.

3. The AC symbol in a schematic is a circle with an AC cycle inside.

4. Other forms of resistance in an AC circuit can be those produced by inductors, capacitors or both.

5. Capacitors and inductors produce a resistance to chances in AC current flow called reactance.

Worksheet 12
Chapter 2, Section 5

1. This means that the wave form position start and stop at different times.

2. They are measured in degrees of equivalent positions of each other. For example a waveform that starts from zero and another wave form starts 90 degrees later, than it would be referenced as a 90 degree phase shift.

3. When the two wave forms are exactly 180 degrees apart, then the signals will cancel each other.

4. Waveform A leads Waveform B in this diagram.

Worksheet 13
Chapter 2, Section 6

1. An RCL circuit is one that contains at least one; resistor, capacitor and indictor.

2. RCL circuit can only operate in an AC circuit. Any DC voltage applied and the circuit will cease to flow because of the high impedance of the capacitor.

3. Each of the components in an RCL circuit produce resistance to current flow measured in Ohms.

4. Resistance to current flow in a RCL caused by the inductor and capacitor is called impedance.

5. The impedance for capacitance and inductance is exactly out of phase.

6. A resistor will provide resistance in phase with the applied signal.

7. The unit of measure of an inductor is a Henry.

8. The resistance to current flow in an AC circuit is called inductance reactance.

9. The inductor will inhibit current flow until the inductors magnetic field is fully charged.

10. The four factors that can control the capacity of a inductor are; the number of turns of the coil, the material of the core (permeability) , the cross section area of the coils and the length of the coil.

11. The purpose of the high permeability core is to direct the magnetic fields of the coil with less loss of field strength.

12. A capacitor can store energy in an electrostatic field, and they pass AC voltage while blocking DC.

13. The difference between a battery and a capacitor is that a capacitor can only store an electrical field while a battery can generate one chemically.

14. The unit of measure of a capacitor is the Farad.

15. A capacitor is constructed of two plates of a conductive material set apart from each other separated by a non-conducting material called a dielectric.

16. Reactance is the imaginary resistance to current flow caused by either the capacitor or inductor and its unit of measure is Ohm Ω.

17. There are two types of reactance in RCL circuits, Inductance Reactance X_L and Capacitance Reactance X_C.

18. When the series circuit's reactance plot is vertical the circuit is purely inductive.

19. The mathematical formula for X_L is: $X_L = 2 \pi f L$

20. Solve for X_L

$$X_L = 2 \pi f L$$
$$X_L = 2 \pi (400)(60)$$
$$X_L = 6.28 \times 400 \times 60$$
$$X_L = 150720$$

$$X_L = 150.7K$$

21. Solve for X_L:

$$X_L = 2 \pi f L$$
$$X_L = 6.28 \times 60K \times 20m$$
$$X_L = 6.28 \times 60000 \times 0.02$$
$$X_L = 7536$$

$$X_L = 7.5K$$

Worksheet 14

Chapter 2, Section 6

1. The sum of the inductive reactance is equal to the total inductive reactance in a series circuit. $X_{L1} + X_{L2} + X_{L3} = X_{LT}$

2. The X_L for each inductor needs to be determined first, then solve for total reactance.

3. Solve for X_{LT}

$X_L = 2 \pi f L$
$X_L = 6.28 \times 120 \times 0.02$ $X_L = 15\Omega$
$X_L = 15\Omega$

First solve for X_L then solve for total X_L in the circuit

$X_L = 2 \pi f L$
$X_L = 6.28 \times 120 \times 0.04$ $X_L = 30.1\Omega$
$X_L = 30.1\Omega$

$X_{LT} = X_{L1} + X_{L2}$
$X_{LT} = 15 \Omega + 30.1\Omega$ $X_{LT} = 45.1\Omega$
$X_{LT} = 45.1\Omega$

4. Solve for X_{LT};

$X_L = 2 \pi f L$
$X_L = 6.28 \times 400 \times 360$ $X_L = 904.3K\Omega$
$X_L = 904320$

First solve for X_L then solve for total X_L in the circuit

$X_L = 2 \pi f L$
$X_L = 6.28 \times 400 \times 480$ $X_L = 1.2M\Omega$
$X_L = 1205760$

$X_{LT} = X_{L1} + X_{L2}$
$X_{LT} = 904320 + 1205760$ $X_{LT} = 2.11M\Omega$
$X_{LT} = 2110080$

5. Total Inductive reactance in a parallel circuit is computed using the same methods as resistance in any parallel circuit.

6. Solve for X_{LT}:

$\dfrac{20 \times 40}{20 + 40} = 13.33$ $\dfrac{25 \times 15}{25 + 15} = 9.37$

$X_{LT} = 5.5 \ \Omega$

$\dfrac{13.33 \times 9.37}{13.33 + 9.37} = \dfrac{124.9}{22.7} = 5.5$

7. Mutual inductance is where voltage can be induced into another separate set of coils by virtue of the second set of coils is in position to receive the magnetic field of the first.

8. Mutual Inductance occurs between the primary coil which in turn conducts voltage into the secondary coil.

9. Because of the delay on the buildup in the coils of the inductor, the current will always be out of phase with the input which will then further adjust the phase of the secondary.

Worksheet 15

Chapter 2, Section 6

1. The circuit is referred to as being capacitate reactance when the plot is less than zero. ($X_C < 0$)

2. The mathematical formula for capacitance reactance. $X_C = \dfrac{1}{2\pi f C}$

3. X_C is inversely proportional to both frequency and capacitance.

4. Solve for X_C:

$$X_c = \frac{1}{2\pi f C} \qquad X_c = \frac{1}{0.000628319}$$

$$X_c = \frac{1}{6.28 \times 50 \times 0.000002} \qquad X_c = 1591.58 \qquad X_c = 1.59K \ \Omega$$

5. Solve for X_C:

$$X_c = \frac{1}{2\pi f C} \qquad X_c = \frac{1}{0.003769911}$$

$$X_c = \frac{1}{6.28 \times 120 \times 0.000005} \qquad X_c = 265.25 \qquad X_c = 265.25 \ \Omega$$

6. Mathematical formula for X_{CT} for capacitors in a series circuit:

$$X_{CT} = X_{C1} + X_{C2} + X_{C3} + \ldots\ldots X_{CN}$$

7. Solve for X_{CT};

$$\frac{1}{X_{CT}} = \frac{1}{X} + \frac{1}{X} + \frac{1}{X}$$

$$\frac{1}{X_{CT}} = \frac{1}{21} + \frac{1}{42} + \frac{1}{42}$$

$$\frac{1}{X_{CT}} = 0.047619048 + 0.023809524 + 0.023809524$$

$$X_{CT} = \frac{1}{0.047619048 + 0.023809524 + 0.023809524}$$

$$X_{CT} = 10.5$$

Worksheet 16

Chapter 2, Section 6

1. The plots that are being measured are the applied voltage (E) and Current (I).

2. In an RCL plot for Voltage and Current, Voltage is normally much higher than the current but they are always in phase.

3. The resistors current and voltage plot is in phase with the applied voltage and current.

4. The maximum amount of phase differential in any plot is 180 degrees, which would be a total cancel of that signal.

5. In an RCL circuit the plots for current will be common for all of the components. (Rule for series circuits).

6. ELI the ICE man helps you remember the relationship between voltage and current of the capacitor and inductor. This put the symbol for the inductor (I) or the capacitor (C) between Voltage (E) or Current (I).

7. The total measure of all of the resistances in an RCL circuit is Impedance (Z).

8. The positive or negative vector of impedance determines if the circuit is more capacitive reactant or inductive reactant.

9. Solve for Z:

First Determine X_C and X_L $X_c = \dfrac{1}{2\pi f C}$ $X_L = 2\pi f L$

$X_c = \dfrac{1}{2 \times \pi \times 60 \times 0.003}$ $X_L = 2 \times \pi \times 60 \times 5$

$X_c = 884.19$ $X_L = 1.88K$

Then Determine Z

$$Z = \sqrt{R^2 + (X_c - X_L)^2}$$

$$Z = \sqrt{10^2 + (884.19 - 1880)^2}$$

$$Z = \sqrt{100 + 991637.5561}$$

$$Z = \sqrt{991737.5561}$$

$$Z = 1K$$

10. Solve for Z:

First Determine X_C and X_L $X_c = \dfrac{1}{2\pi f C}$ $X_L = 2\pi f L$

$X_c = \dfrac{1}{2 \times \pi \times 2000 \times 0.000006}$ $X_L = 2 \times \pi \times 2000 \times 0.002$

$X_c = 13.26M\Omega$ $X_L = 25.13\Omega$

Then Determine Z

$$Z = \sqrt{R^2 + (X_c - X_L)^2}$$

$$Z = \sqrt{25^2 + (13260000 - 25.13)^2}$$

$$Z = \sqrt{625 + 175826933553031.5}$$

$$Z = \sqrt{175826933553656.5}$$

$$Z = 13.26M\Omega$$

Worksheet 17

Chapter 2, Section 6

1. Voltage is common through each of the components in a parallel RCL circuit.

2. In a parallel RCL, current is the variable that will indicate the plot for impedance in the circuit.

3. Solve for Z and I_T:

   First we need to find the current in each branch. I_R I_{XL} I_{XC}

   $I_R = E/R$ $I_R = 110/50$ $I_R = 2.2a$

   Next solve for X_C and X_L

   $X_c = \dfrac{1}{2\pi f C}$ $X_L = 2\pi f L$

   $X_c = \dfrac{1}{2 \times \pi \times 60 \times 0.000012}$ $X_L = 2 \times \pi \times 60 \times 5$

   $X_c = \dfrac{1}{0.004523893}$

   $X_c = 221.05$ $X_L = 1885$

   Solve for current in each branch

   $I_c = E/X$ $I_c = 110/221.05$ $I_c = 0.497a$

   $I_L = E/X$ $I_L = 110/1885$ $I_L = 0.058a$

   Then solve for current total

   $I_T = \sqrt{I_R^2 + (I_c - I_L)^2}$ $I_T = \sqrt{2.2^2 + (0.497 - 0.058)^2}$

   $I_T = \sqrt{4.84 + 0.192721}$

   $I_T = \sqrt{5.032721}$ $I_T = 2.24a$

   Last solve for Z $Z = E_A/I_T$ $Z = 110/2.24$ $Z = 49.1$

4. Solve for Z and I_T:

   First we need to find the current in each branch. I_R I_{XL} I_{XC}

   $I_R = E/R$ $I_R = 28/40$ $I_R = 0.7a$

   Next solve for X_C and X_L

   $X_c = \dfrac{1}{2\pi f C}$ $X_L = 2\pi f L$

   $X_c = \dfrac{1}{2 \times \pi \times 140 \times .000006}$ $X_L = 2 \times \pi \times 140 \times 0.02$

   $X_c = \dfrac{1}{0.005277876}$

   $X_c = 189.47$ $X_L = 17.59$

   Solve for current in each branch

   $I_c = E/X_c$ $I_c = 28/189.47$ $I_c = 0.147a$

   $I_L = E/X_L$ $I_L = 28/17.59$ $I_L = 1.592a$

   Then solve for current total

   $I_T = \sqrt{I_R^2 + (I_c - I_L)^2}$ $I_T = \sqrt{0.7^2 + (0.147 - 1.592)^2}$

   $I_T = \sqrt{0.49 + 2.088}$

   $I_T = \sqrt{2.578}$ $I_T = 1.6a$

   Last solve for Z $Z = E_A/I_T$ $Z = 28/1.6a$ $Z = 17.5$

Worksheet 18

Chapter 2, Section 6

1. Resonance is when the inductance and capacitance reactance in a circuit is equal.

2. The input frequency is what allows a circuit to operate at Resonance.

3. The value of the capacitor and the value of the inductor determine at what frequency resonance occurs.

4. In a series RCL circuit, current is at minimum and Impedance is at maximum.

5. The H_{PP} is position A

6. The distance between A and C is the bandwidth for this plot.

7. Item D is the determination of the Half Power points of this plot. This is when the overall plot reaches .707 of the maximum current.

8. The bandwidth for this plot is 4Mhz. (126Mhz – 122Mhz)

9. Solve for Resonance Frequency:

$$f_r = \frac{1}{2\pi\sqrt{LC}} \quad f_r = \frac{1}{2\pi\sqrt{0.05 \times 0.000006}}$$

$$\sqrt{0.0000003}$$

$$f_r = \frac{1}{2\pi \times 0.000547723}$$

$$f_r = \frac{1}{0.003441442}$$

$$f_r = 290.57Hz$$

10. Solve for Resonance Frequency:

$$f_r = \frac{1}{2\pi\sqrt{LC}} \quad f_r = \frac{1}{2\pi\sqrt{10 \times 0.000015}}$$

$$\sqrt{0.00015}$$

$$f_r = \frac{1}{2\pi \times 0.012247448}$$

$$f_r = \frac{1}{0.0769139779}$$

$$f_r = 13KHz$$

11. Q in a circuit refers to the quality of the operation of a circuit at resonance. The bandwidth of a circuit determines the Q.

12. Q is classified as either High Q with a tall and narrow bandwidth and low Q with a low and wide bandwidth.

Worksheet 19

Chapter 2, Section 6

1. The difference is that at resonance frequency in parallel RCL , the impedance in the circuit will be at minimum while the current will be at maximum.

2. Another name for a tank circuit is the frequency determining device (FDD) in an oscillator.

3. A tank circuit needs DC voltage to start the oscillations.

4. A tank circuit operates by the two devices charging and discharging into each other at a prescribed frequency.

5. The oscillation cycle is called a flywheel effect.

6. If the tank circuit does not receive any new voltage, the wave of the output will dampen. This is where the frequency remains constant but the amplitude decreases.

7. The dampening wave is caused by energy loss due to the resistance in the circuit.

8. To maintain amplitude in the tank circuit regenerative feedback needs to be added.

Worksheet 20

Chapter 2, Section 7

1. The two parts of a transformer are the primary and the secondary windings.

2. A transformer is designed to transform one voltage value to another.

3. When the value of voltage is stepped up in a transformer the current in the circuit must decrease.

4. When voltage is stepped down in a transformer, the current will increase.

5. When the primary voltage is 120 and the resultant voltage is 60, this makes the ratio 2:1 which is a step down transformer. (120/60)

6. The input of the primary is 10 times the secondary; this puts the output as a multiple of the input. (10 x 60 = 600 volts) The input is then 600volts.

7. The ratio for this transformer is 1 to 2.5 which places this as a step up transformer. But remember that current is directly opposite of the voltage in a transformer. (2.5/50 = 0.05a or 50mA)

8. If the primary is 30 and the secondary is 900 then the ratio is divided (30/900 = 1 to 30)

9. The voltage of the primary is 45 then the secondary voltage is 135 in a 3:1 transformer.

$$\frac{V_P}{V_S} = \frac{N_P}{N_S}$$

$$\frac{45}{X} = \frac{300}{900} \quad \frac{45}{X} = \frac{1}{3} \quad X=135\text{Volts}$$

Worksheet 21
Chapter 3, Section 1

1. Pure semiconductor material actually has very poor conducting properties.

2. So a semiconductor can be made to conduct electrons at a desired condition, the material must be mixed with impurities. This is called doping the material.

3. N-type semiconductor material is created when as the silicon is grown it is doped with a phosphorous, arsenic or antimony that creates an excess of electrons in the semiconductor.

4. The electrical property of P-type material is that it has an excess of holes, which accepts the electrons from the N-material when charged.

5. The standard electrical symbol for a standard diode.

6. Forward bias in a diode is when the diode is conducting electricity.

7. If current is applied to the anode end (-) then the electrons backup against the N-material and the current is blocked. This condition is called reverse bias.

Worksheet 22
Chapter 3, Section 2

1. When AC current is passed through a diode it rectifies the voltage.

2. The P-type part of the diode is called the anode and the cathode is the N-type.

3. The diode is marked on the cathode with a stripe.

4. For a Germanium Silicon diode it takes at least 0.7volts to start current flowing in forward bias.

5. The diode will block the reverse biascurrent until it reaches the breakdown voltage.

6. No a silicon diode will heat up and fracture and fail when in reverse bias too long.

7. Diodes are used in AM radio signals to help in receiving the audio, they are used in circuits to rectify the AC signal into a DC voltage to drive a speaker.

8. The peak voltage minus the push voltage of the diode then 70% of that equals the RMS voltage.

$$5Vac - 0.7Vac = 4.3V \text{ peak}$$
$$4.3V \times .707 = 3 V_{RMS}$$

Worksheet 23
Chapter 3, Section 3

1. Rectification is a process where the negative polarity of an input signal is electrically filtered out.

2. If an audio signal is not rectified the human ear would hear both the negative and positive peaks which would cancel out the sound.

3. A single diode is called a half wave rectifier.

4. A bridge rectifier is called a full wave rectifier because the full wave conducts all of the time at the output.

5. A Bridge Rectifier has four diodes drawn in a square. All of the diodes need to "point" in one direction. The input is connected directly across from the output.

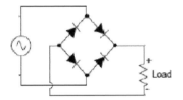

Worksheet 24
Chapter 3, Section 3

1. The voltage waveform from a full wave rectifier is called ripple voltage.

2. A choke inductor is connected in series to the output of the load.

3. For a capacitor to function as a filter it must be placed in parallel to the output load.

4. The choke inductor resists the change in current of the input averaging the waveform.

5. When the AC signal lowers to a level less than the voltage of the stored energy of the capacitor, the voltage then comes from the capacitor to the load.

6. A Pi filter contains two shunt capacitors and a choke inductor in series between.

7. A bleeder resistor is also called a safety resistor than drains both capacitors when the load is removed,

Worksheet 25
Chapter 3, Section 3

1. A variactor is a device used for filters, oscillators and amplifiers where high frequency operation is required,

2. The variable capacitance of this device is created by the width of the depletion zones in the diode that causes changes in electrical potential the same way a capacitor does.
3. A variactor is designed to operate in reverse bias.
4. When the reverse bias voltage decreases the capacitor value in the variactor increases.
5. If the reverse bias voltage is increased to high the breakdown voltage is reached which will stop the variactor from functioning.

Worksheet 26

Chapter 3, Section 3

$$I_{R1} = \frac{V_S - V_Z}{R_1} \qquad \frac{50-28}{550} = 40mA$$

1. The forward bias voltage of a geranium diode is .7 of a volt.
2. A voltage regulator diode operates in the reverse bias direction which conducts only when the avalanche voltage is reached.
3. The resistor R_1 is the current limiting for D1 when current begins to flow.
4. The resistor R_3 used for the load resistance for the output.
5. Voltage regulating diodes will create heat as they operate. This will have a negative coefficient which will change the zener output voltage.
6. A Schottkey diode has a metallic junction that will allow for faster voltage recovery which in turn will allow it to better operate in high frequencies.
7. The Schotkey diode diagram in a circuit and a Zener

 Cathode — Anode Zener

8. A voltage regulator diode the set voltage is the breakdown of the depletion zone in reverse bias
9. Diodes operating in either forward or reverse bias have zero effect on current.
10. A zener diode is constructed in a way that its breakdown voltage can be varied based on the size of the depletion zones.
11. The voltage drop across the Load is 1.5Volts due to the large drop across R_2.
12. A Schottkey diode has a metallic junction for the N material.
13. The metal junction that allows for high frequency operation.

Worksheet 27

Chapter 3, Section 4

1. An electronic voltage regulator is based on a diode that is conducting in its avalanche region.
2. The construction of the PN junction determines the zener so this will be determined by the technician as the diodes labeled zener voltage.
3. IR1 is the current limiting resistor for the zener branch to prevent a short.
4. To determine this you will need this formula:

$$=.04A \text{ or } 40mA \qquad I_{R1} = \frac{V_S - V_Z}{R_1}$$

5. To determine the current of the load you need this formula:

$$I = \frac{V_{RL}}{R_L} \quad \frac{28}{300} = 93mA$$

6. In this situation the input voltage has dropped below the zener voltage. This means that the load and the series resistor are in series and voltage will continue to drop.
7. When there is a changing load the series resistor must be changed to prevent a reduction in the bias of the zener diode.
8. A series transistor is placed in the circuit to the load to act as a variable resistance by having the bias voltage varied after the zener diode.
9. Forward Bias for the Q1 is from the voltage across R_1 minus the .6 of a volt required to start the transistor to flow.
10. When the input voltage drops, the zener voltage will remain the same after the diode. However the voltage across R_1 drops. This in turn drops the forward bias into the transistor which increase the voltage drops for the load proportional to the increase in input voltage.
11. For the Electronic Voltage Regulator (EVR) there are four major paths for current flow that parallel the load and the input.
12. The transistor Q_1 controls current by varying the voltage drop in series to the load resistor.
13. The resistor R_1 is the current controlling device for the Zener diode CR1.
14. When an input voltage is first applied, it is sensed at the voltage divider. This will cause changes in bias to Q_1 and Q_2 which adjust to both changes to input voltage and load current changes.
15. The change in the forward bias of Q_2 causes a decrease in the voltage drop. This in turn causes an increase in the forward bias of Q_1. The reduction of the resistance causes a reduction of voltage drop to the load proportional to the change in the input.
16. Moving the wiper arm down causes the forward bias of Q_2 down which in turn causes an increase of the forward bias of Q_1 which will reduces the voltage drop across the transistor allowing the load voltage to increase.

Worksheet 28
Chapter 3, Section 4

1. Transistors are semiconductor devices that replaced glass electron tubes.

2. A BJT transistor is named because it contains two PNP or NPN junctions in its construction.

3. Three junctions of a transistor is identified as Base Collector and Emitter.

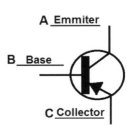

A Emmiter

B Base

C Collector

4. The two junction types are as shown.

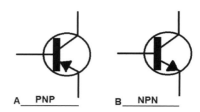

A PNP   B NPN

5. Diagram showing the current flow through the transistor.

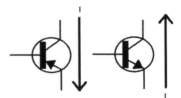

6. To encourage current directionality in a transistor, manufacturers dope the emitters and collectors slightly differently to encourage forward and reverse bias operations.

7. A transistor will operate in three electrical conditions, Cutoff, Saturation and Linear (Dynamic).

8. When a transistor is being used as a switch, it is being cycled between cutoff and saturation.

9. The percentage of current flow of this device is the Collector/Emitter junction is 95 to 99% and the collector/base junction is 1 to 5%.

10. For the diagram at right, the circuit is at cutoff because the Collector/Base junction is open.

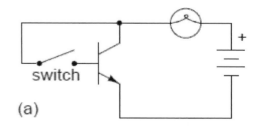

switch

(a)

Worksheet 29

Chapter 3, Section 6

1. The purpose of an amplifier is to increase the signal amplitude of either signal or power.

2. An amplifier is constructed of a signal input such as a microphone or RF receiver, a DC power supply, an output device such as a speaker or another circuit and a semiconductor transistor.

3. When DC voltage is supplied the PN junctions have wide depletion zones and no current is flowing through the transistor.

4. The input signal is applied to the base of the transistor.

5. When the signal is applied to the base in a BJT, the depletion zones change and the current flow in the same pattern as the input signal

6. The types of transistors used in amplifiers in addition to the Bipolar Junction (BJT) there is a Field Effect Transistor (FET) and a Junction Field Effect (JFET) which can be enhanced with metal-oxide, this is called a (MOSFET).

7. The FET have a source and drain that is connected to the amplifier input power supply and a gate which applies a negative voltage potential to control the flow in the transistor output.

8. The MOSFET have two zones of N material connected to the source and drain embedded in P material.

9. The transistor is functioning as a variable resistor in an amplifier.

10. There has to be a resistor in the same lead as the source voltage because there can be times when the transistors resistance becomes effectively zero. Without a resistor, it could cause as short to ground of the power supply.

11. The output for a standard amplifier is taken across the emitter junction and ground. This is similar to taking voltage across a variable resistor.

12. The gain of an amplifier is the total of the signal input and the applied voltage minus the loss of the gain resistor.

Worksheet 30
Chapter 3, Section 7

1. When configuring the three types, the common connection is that the grounds are common with the base, collector or emitter.

2. A is common collector, B is common Emitter and C is common base.

3. Bias is when you add a positive voltage to the input to keep the current in the transistor continuously flowing.

4. Bias voltage in the amplifier can affect the class of operation of the amplifier.

5. For a true amplifier, the output of the single is 180 degrees out of phase.

6. For a pure replication of the input there has to be enough *forward bias* to keep the current in the emitter junction flowing all the time.

7. In the forward bias is developed by R_1 and R_2.

8. C1 is used to couple the input to the amplifier to where only an AC signal will pass.

9. The output or the gain of the amplifier is controlled by R_3.

10. The input is 180 degrees out of phase to the output.

11. The VCC is the DC supply voltage that is used to amplify the output.

12. R4 helps compensate for the loss of resistance that is causes by the transistor heating up.

13. This is a common emitter amplifier.

Worksheet 31
Chapter 3, Section 7

1. Static operation is where the input signal is zero and the only increase is any bias voltage that is added to the base.

2. The voltage path for static bias is sent through the collector then out the base.

3. Dynamic operation of an amplifier is where the current in the emitter junction varies with the input waveform.

Worksheet 32
Chapter 3, Section 7

1. The characteristic graph plots the vertical scale which is the I_C (collector current) compared to the V_{CE} (collector voltage)

2. The line in the graph between point A and B represent the saturation (B) and cutoff (A).

3. Cutoff is the maximum amount of voltage applied to the amplifier.

4. Saturation is the maximum amount of current that could possibly flow in the Collector junction.

5. The "Q" point of the plot is the exact optimum position of an amplifier output between cutoff and saturation.

6. Gain is the amount of amplification of a signal. This could be a peak voltage or an average voltage.

7. Bias refers to how much of the waveform is amplified before it reaches either cutoff or saturation.

8. Q is determined by knowing how much current can flow in the base junction when the value of all of the circuit resistance is totaled.

9. Gain is inversely proportional to the output of the amplifier. This means as the resistances of the gain resistor increases, the output of the amplifier decreases.

$$\text{Gain} = \frac{\triangle \text{Output}}{\triangle \text{ Input}}$$

10. Gain is described as the change in the output over the change of the input.

11. Changing R3 controls both the Gain and Bias which changes the operation of the amplifier.

Worksheet 33
Chapter 3, Section 7

1. The four classes of amplifier operation are; A, AB, B and C.

2. The classes of operation are comparing fidelity to efficiency.

3. A class A amplifier gives the best fidelity but with the lowest efficiency.

4. A class AB amplifier conducts 99 to 50 percent of the time which preserves some fidelity.

5. A class C amplifier is used primarily for power amplification.

6. A buffer amplifier is used for impedance matching.

7. The buffer amplifier gain is less than one.

8. The R_1 resistor determines the forward bias.

9. The output gain of this amplifier is taken from the collector junction which makes the output gain of this amplifier less than 1.

10. This amplifier is used for impedance matching of the next circuit of the output of the high impedance output of an oscillator.

Worksheet 34
Chapter 3, Section 7

1. This refers to that; as a transistor current increases, the resistance of the transistor will decrease.

2. As the temperature of the transistor increases the resistance could move the amplifier above its operating point (saturation).

3. The swamping resistor is placed at the emitter for the transistor to pull back on the collector current.

4. A bypass capacitor is placed across the swamping resistor to allow current to pass without distortion during low load conditions.

5. The thermistor will change its resistance value as the transistor heats up then reducing the forward bias of the transistor.

6. Diodes are manufactured from the same semiconductor materials as the transistor and therefore their internal resistance follows closely as the temperature increases.

7. Double diode installations are used for hard working amplifiers to make sure that one diode remains forward bias at all times.

8. A heat sink is used to directly radiate heat away from the transistor using cooling fins.

Worksheet 35
Chapter 3, Section 7

1. A cascade amplifier allows the signal to obtain large gains with minimal distortion.

2. A direct coupling is the only one that can pass a DC voltage.

3. The RL coupling has the most high frequency loss because of the X_L of the inductor at higher frequencies.

4. In an LC coupler, the gain of the amplifier is controlled by the resonance frequency of the inductor and capacitor.

5. RC couplers have very low frequency responses because of the capacitor.

6. Because there is no physical connection, between stages, the transformer coupling is the best to prevent circuit feedback.

7. Transformer = D

8. Direct = A

9. LC = C

10. RC = B

Worksheet 36
Chapter 3, Section 7

1. Before oscillators, radio signals used OOK (on off keying) to modulate the signal in Morse code.

2. The primary purpose of an oscillator is to produce a high frequency signal with consistent frequency and amplitude.

3. The four main components of an oscillator are: a DC voltage supply, a frequency determining device, an amplifier and a regenerative feedback loop.

4. The output requirement of any oscillator is a stable frequency and stable amplitude.

5. The value of the capacitor and the inductor as a frequency determining device determines the output of the oscillator based on the resonance frequency of those two devices.

6. Regenerative feedback is a measure of the output amplitude of the FDD which is fed to the forward bias of the amplifier causing energy to be fed back into the FDD to maintain its amplitude.

7. Resonance is the frequency that the tank circuits of the FDD flywheels.

8. Resistors R1 and R2 provide the bias voltage for the amplifier.

9. The FDD is L1, L2 and C3.

10. Changing the variable capacitor C3 can change the output of the oscillator.

11. The regenerative feedback loop starts at Q1 through L1 and L2 then through C2 to the base of Q1.

12. Swamping resistor R3 with by-pass capacitor C1 make up the thermal stabilization circuit of the oscillator.

13. To isolate the DC power supply from the output, a capacitor C4 is placed at ground near the power supply.

14. To prevent feedback from the oscillator, the output is coupled to a transformer.

Worksheet 37
Chapter 3, Section 7

1. Impedance is the out of phase elements between the impedance of the inductors and capacitors. High impedance is where the phase difference is large enough to cause a loss of power transfer for the oscillator.

2. The buffer amplifier couples the input of the amplifier to the base of the transistor but outputs the amplifier off of the emitter junction. This does not change the output load but reduces impedance by matching the input to the output.

3. The overall gain of a buffer amplifier is less than one.

4. A frequency multiplier is a special class C amplifier.

5. When the forward bias is driven higher toward cutoff, the tops of the waveform gets wider.

6. If the harmonic is multiplied too many times, the signals tend to cancel each other out which will lower the output signal.

7.

Worksheet 38

Chapter 3, Section 7

1. That a crystal has a voltage applied it will electrically oscillate at a specific frequency. This is called the piezoelectric effect.

2. The output frequency of a crystal oscillator is determined by the physical dimensions.

3. Q1 is a common collector and Q2 is a common base amplifier.

4. C1 couples the output of amp Q2 to the base of Q1.

5. The tank circuit does not provide the output frequency but helps to develop the load voltage at the output frequency. This is because at the resonance frequency its impedance is very high cutting off voltage to Q2.

6. Starting at Y1 to the emitter of Q2 out collector to C1 to the Base of Q1 out the emitter of Q1 back to Y1.

7. To change the frequency you need to physically change the crystal.

Worksheet 39

Chapter 3, Section 8

1. A filter is a device that either passes or blocks a selected section of frequencies.

2. A filter can be in either; L-section, T-section or Pie-section

3. An electronic filter is made up of capacitors and inductors in various configurations.

4. A filter is made up of a series component and a shunt component. The output is taken (developed) off of the shunt component.

5. A band reject filter.

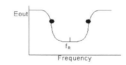

6. Low pass Filter.

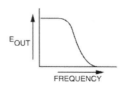

7. Band pass filter.

8. High Pass Filter.

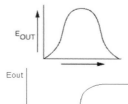

Worksheet 40

Chapter 3, Section 10

1. An OpAmp can produce either inverting or non-inverting output for a buffer amplifier.

2. An OpAmp produces a very high gain with a high impedance to a lower output impedance.

3. When a portion of the input is re-fed back into the input in phase this is an example of regenerative feedback.

4. When out of phase or negative feedback is placed at the output destructive interference occurs.

Worksheet 41

Chapter 3, Section 10

1. A sawtooth wave generator is simply a resistor and capacitor where the RC time constant determines the rate of charge and the breakdown of the capacitor.

2. Mulitvibrator circuits come in monostable, astable and bistable varieties.

3. The maximum length of the square wave in a oneshot multivibrator is determined by the charging rate of the capacitor.

4. To determine the Pulse Recurrence Frequency (PRF) you divide the Pulse Recurrence Time (PRT) by 1/PRT=PRF

5. A SR Flip Flop is a two state device which outputs two opposite signals. For example is one output is labeled Q then the other will be Not Q.

6. An Astable multivibrator produces a rhythmic square wave generator based on the fact that the two parts of the circuit conducts at only one time.

7. Due to the fact that only one capacitor can charge at a time the opposite transistor bias is held at negative while the other is charging.

8. The resistor R3 and R9 determine the charge time for C3 and C4.

9. To adjust the frequency of the oscillator you would need to adjust R5 up or down.

10. An Astable multivibrator produces a square or rectangle wave.

11. The discharge path for capacitor C3 is R7, R6,R5 Q1 then out D1.

12. The time to cutoff for Q1 will decrease.

Worksheet 42
Chapter 4, Section 1

1. The two classifications of batteries are primary and secondary.

2. A primary battery cannot be recharged.

3. The electrodes of a primary battery are constructed of carbon (anode) and zinc (cathode).

4. An atom or molecule that has a positive or negative charge is called an ion.

5. The electrons will flow to and from the electrodes is called the electrolyte.

6. A typical dry cell battery will produce 1.5 Volts.

7. Lead acid battery will produce sulfate on the plates when left in a discharge state for too long.

8. The two main elements that make up a NiCad battery are Nickel and Cadmium.

9. The Ni-Cad battery can hold its maximum voltage longer before fully discharging.

10. Ni-Cad batteries are susceptible to thermal runaway during charging.

11. With no load applied a voltage meter would read open circuit voltage (OCV)

12. When using the formula:

$$IR=\frac{OCV-CCV}{Load} \qquad \frac{14.2-11.6}{85} = 30mA$$

13. In aircraft there can be vented cell batteries and recombinant gas (sealed) batteries.

14. Batteries connected in series will increase the voltage while holding the ampere down.

Worksheet 43
Chapter 4, Section 1

1. A lead acid battery is 70% water and 30% sulfuric acid by weight.

2. For lead acid battery plates antimony is added to hardened the plates.

3. Aviation battery vent caps are self sealing when tipped to prevent spillage.

4. When a voltage is measured from a battery when it is connected to a circuit it is measuring the state of charge of a battery while a voltage taken of a battery out of the aircraft is only measuring the maximum voltage of the battery.

5. A recombinant gas battery is one that recombines the vent gasses therefore does not require venting.

6. Aviation batteries are made up of individual cells connected in series.

7. As lead acid battery charge and discharge they lose some of the lead material into the solution which can short out the cells.

8. When removing a battery from an aircraft it is important to remove the negative cable first.

9. For testing the state of charge of a lead/acid battery, a technician would use a hydrometer.

10. The two types of battery chargers are the constant-current and the constant-voltage.

11. A constant-current charger should not be connected to an actual aircraft because of temperature and venting issues.

Worksheet 44

Chapter 4, Section 2

1. Mechanical switches are named by the number of poles (the pivot portion) and the throw (the fixed contact).

2. A toggle switch is usually those having a single throw and pole.

3. A multi-throw switch is one that may have a single pivot point that can connect to one of many choices.

4. Momentary on switches can be used for push to talks, attendant call, ground call or microphone transmit button on a hand microphone.

5. Solve.

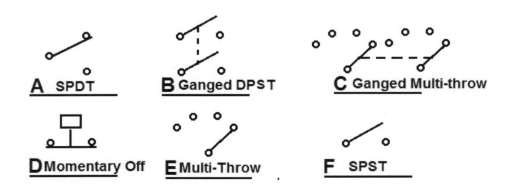

A SPDT

B Ganged DPST

C Ganged Multi-throw

D Momentary Off

E Multi-Throw

F SPST

Worksheet 45

Chapter 4, Section 2

1. A relay is a device that uses a small amount of electrical energy to control a larger one.

2. The armature is the only moving part of a relay.

3. An electromagnet pulls the armature onto the core.

4. There will be a set of normally open and a set of normally closed contacts.

5. A broken spring might cause the relay not to retract or disconnect.

6. A solenoid is a very rugged relay that can handle high current loads.

7. An overload relay is used in circuit breaker applications.

8. Relays have three basic sections that could cause a malfunction the, coil, contacts and mechanical section.

9. If a coil is reading infinity or open, the coil is open and will not operate.

10. Refer to the diagram below and give the multimeter reading in volts between the test point and ground.

     a. Pin 7 _____0 Volts_____
     b. Pin 5 _____0 Volts_____
     c. Pin 8 ___115 Volts___
     d. Pin 2 ____25 Volts____
     e. Pin 3 ___115 Volts___
     f. Pin 1 _____0 Volts_____

Worksheet 46

Chapter 4, Section 2

1. Proximity sensors operate using mutual inductance.

2. Placing a steel target next to a proximity sensor changes the X_L of the device which is sensed by circuits.

3. Fuel probes of large aircraft are constructed like large capacitors with the fuel acting as the dielectric.

4. The probes are wired in parallel so they can give an accurate fuel level in a tank at any attitude.

5. A bimetallic junction is two dissimilar metal are bonded together to form a bond that will bend under a temperature change.

6. Alumel and Chromel junction will produce voltage when heated.

7. A position sensor is one that uses an electrical signal to represent an indication of actuated components such as flaps, landing gear, leading edge devices, etc. in the cockpit.

8. The problem with using a single resistor as a position indicator is that the calibration is adversely effected by variances in system voltage.

9. To provide accurate variable resistance reading of an indicator, a resistor bridge circuit is used.

Worksheet 47
Chapter 4, Section 3

1. 25_{10} = 11001_2 Bin $\qquad$ 31_8 Oct = 19_{16} Hex

2. 102_{10} = 1100110_2 Bin $\qquad$ 146_8 Oct = 66_{16} Hex

3. 86_{10} = 1010110_2 Bin $\qquad$ 126_8 Oct = 56_{16} Hex

4. 135_{10} = 10000111_2 Bin $\qquad$ = 207_8 Oct = 87_{16} Hex

5. 281_{10} = 100011001_2 Bin $\qquad$ = 431_8 Oct = 119_{16} Hex

6. 44_{10} = 101100_2 Bin $\qquad$ = 54_8 Oct = $2C_{16}$ Hex

7. 1001_{10} = 1111101001_2 Bin $\qquad$ = 1751_8 Oct = $3E9_{16}$ Hex

8. 222_{10} = 11011110_2 Bin $\qquad$ = 336_8 Oct = DE_{16} Hex

Worksheet 48
Chapter 4, Section 3
Addition

1.
```
   1 1   1
    110001
  +  11001
   1001010
```

2.
```
   1   1
   100100
 + 110100
  1011000
```

3.
```
   1 1 1 1
   100100
 + 111111
  1100011
```

4.
```
    11000
  +   111
    11111
```

5.
```
   1 1 1 1 1
     10101
  +   1111
    100100
```

6.
```
       1
    10011
  +  1010
    11100
```

198

Subtraction

7.
```
  ̷1 ̷11
   1 11
  ̷10001
 -   110
    1011
```

10.
```
  ̷1 ̷1 1
   11 ̷1
  ̷10001
 -   1 ̷10
    1011
```

8.
```
       ̷1
        1
  11 ̷1001
 -    ̷100
   110101
```

11.
```
    ̷1 1
     1 ̷1
  ̷100111
 -   ̷1000
    11111
```

9.
```
   ̷1 1
    1 ̷1
  ̷1001
 -   ̷11
    110
```

12.
```
    ̷1 ̷1
     11
  1 ̷1001
 -   1 ̷10
    10011
```

Worksheet 49
Chapter 4, Section 3
Multiply

1.
```
      100010
  x       10
      000000
  +1000100
    1000100
```

2.
```
      101010
  x      101
      101010
     0000000
  + 10101000
     11010010
```

3.
```
       111001
  x      1001
       111001
      0000000
     00000000
    111001000
   1000000001
```

4.
```
       101000
  x      1001
       101000
      0000000
     00000000
  + 101000000
    101101000
```

Divide

5.
```
        110
  10⟌1100
       10
       10
       10
       10
       00
```

6.
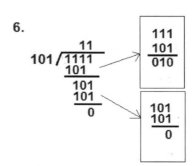
```
        11
  101⟌1111
       101
       101
       101
         0
```

7.

```
         1011
111/1001101
     111
     101
       0
     1010
      111
      111
      111
        0
```

```
  11
 011
 1001
-111
   10
```

```
   1
  1 1
 0 0
1010
 111
  11
```

Worksheet 50

Chapter 4, Section 4

1. The inputs/outputs of a logic circuit or device are either a high 1 or low 0.

2. Logic Gates represent decision actions that are required for circuit operation.

3. Logic Function is the relationship of the output to the inputs.

4. A truth table is used to plot all of the possible outputs against all of the possible input combinations.

5. An AND gate is one were all must be high before a high can be given.

6. A buffer or inverter is a device whose only function is to inverse the input.

7. Adding an inverter to the output of a AND gate make it into a NAND Gate.

8. A logic signal chart is used to plot the actions of various gates over time.

9. A rhythmic signal on a logic signal chart is called the clock pulse.

Worksheet 51

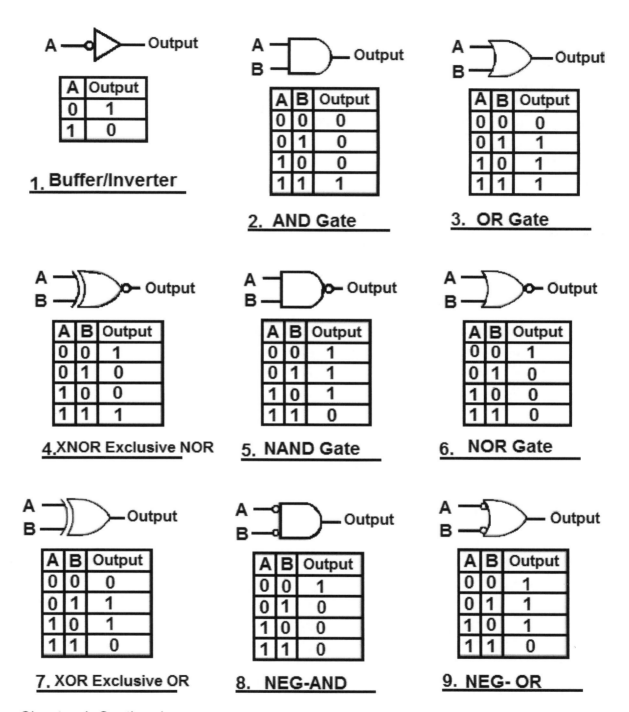

A	Output
0	1
1	0

1. Buffer/Inverter

A	B	Output
0	0	0
0	1	0
1	0	0
1	1	1

2. AND Gate

A	B	Output
0	0	0
0	1	1
1	0	1
1	1	1

3. OR Gate

A	B	Output
0	0	1
0	1	0
1	0	0
1	1	1

4. XNOR Exclusive NOR

A	B	Output
0	0	1
0	1	1
1	0	1
1	1	0

5. NAND Gate

A	B	Output
0	0	1
0	1	0
1	0	0
1	1	0

6. NOR Gate

A	B	Output
0	0	0
0	1	1
1	0	1
1	1	0

7. XOR Exclusive OR

A	B	Output
0	0	1
0	1	0
1	0	0
1	1	0

8. NEG-AND

A	B	Output
0	0	1
0	1	1
1	0	1
1	1	0

9. NEG- OR

Chapter 4, Section 4

Worksheet 52

Chapter 4, Section 4

1. A Flip Flop is a synchronous bi-stable storage device that will store one bit as either a 1 high or 0 low.

2. The diagram shows a S-R Flip-Flop which is a Set Reset.

3. The inputs are a Set connection, Reset connection, a clock input and two outputs that will be opposite of each other.

4. Because this is a Flip-Flop the trigger for signal will happen on the time down beat or up-beat.

5. Should the device receive a S and R at the same time, the device will be unstable and it might switch, it might not.

6. This is a D-type Flip-Flop. This operates based on the input put into D.

7. A low placed at D will set the Q to 0.

8. This is a not Q output that will always be the opposite of Q.

9. Fill out the Truth Table for a J-K Flip Flop.

J	K	C	Q	$\bar{Q}$	Operation
0	0	Rising Edge	—	—	Hold (no Change)
0	1	Rising Edge	0	1	Reset
1	0	Rising Edge	1	0	Set
1	1	Rising Edge	—	—	Toggle

J-K Flip-flop Truth Table

10. With Q at 1 the plot would look like this if Q is started at high:

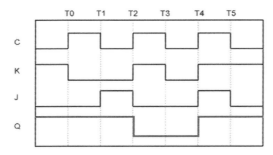

11. The diagram in the picture is a full adder.

12. This diagram is a half adder because it does not have a carry-in input.

13. The logic contains Exclusive OR Gates (2) AND Gates (2) and one OR gate. Inputs A and B are connected to one EX-OR gate and one AND Gate. The output of the first EX-OR is then connected to one of the inputs to the second EX-OR Gate. The Output of the first EX-OR is also connected to one lead of the second AND Gate. The Carry In in then connected to the second input of the second EX-OR. The output of the second AND is then sent to one of the inputs of the last OR Gate. The other connection of the OR Gate receives the output of the first AND Gate. The output of the OR gate will be the Carry Out for the next adder.

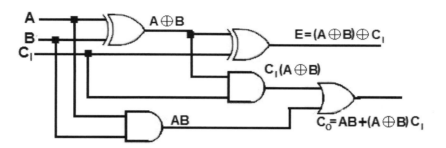

Worksheet 53

Chapter 5, Section 1

1. Aircraft wiring must meet FAA specifications and be installed and maintained in accordance with FAA approved processes. The FAA standards may be referenced industry standards such as MIL Standards or could meet original specifications during aircraft certification.

2. Aircraft wire is designed to be lightweight, corrosion resistant, uniform construction, meet flammability standards (doesn't produce dangerous fumes when burned), and is able to withstand motion and flexing without breaking.

3. Forms of wires are single wires, not generally used in aircraft except for thermocouples, etc. and multiple conductor wire which form cables when they are run concurrently with additional conductors they are termed wire bundles. The properties of these conductors and cables accept soldering and crimping connection well.

4. Two of the best conductors are gold and silver because valence orbits are nearly empty only containing two electrons each. Two of the best insulators are neon and helium because their valences orbits are full.

5. The most common aircraft wire is stranded copper to achieve maximum flexibility. The wire is generally 7 or 19 strands based on the gauge of the wire. The wire is coated to prevent oxidation and promote solderability. The coating materials are rated by their ability to with stand heat generated by the electrical circuit. Tin-Lead is rated up to 105 degrees C, Silver is rated to 200 degrees C and Nickel is rated to 260 degrees C.

6. Insulators are materials that have more than four valence electrons which inhibits electron flow. Insulator material is governed by cost, operating temperature, insulation resistance, abrasion resistance, chemical resistance and strength.

7. Shielding is for radio frequency interference (RFI) both from the wire itself and from outside sources. Shielding does not completely eliminate the RFI but directs the energy to ground.

8. Coaxial cables have some shielding properties as a part of its construction; however the primary concern is to maintain precise dimensions between the conductor and the outer shield to establish precise impedance values. Typically, aircraft coax cables are designed for 50 Ω impedances.

9. Aluminum wire is approved for some aircraft applications where weight reduction is necessary but there several considerations necessary for its application. The minimum size of the wire is #6AWG or larger and special connections are necessary to prevent galvanic corrosion and special hardware to prevent electrolytic corrosion.

10. American Wire Gage (AWG) protocols are used to specify wire diameters. The numbers assigned are inverse to the actual diameters. For example, #20 AWG wire is 0.032 inches in diameter and #0 AWG wire is 0.325 inches in diameter.

11. The wire usage chart is designed for technicians and installers to properly select the correct wire for a specific environment. The chart is published in the FAA Advisory Circular AC 43-13-1B and has complete instruction for its use.

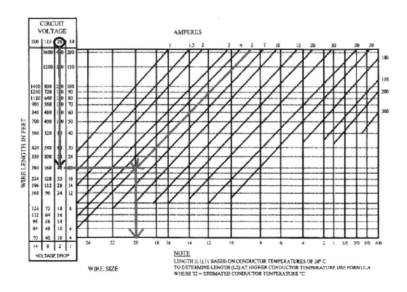

12. Starting at the 28Vdc column draw a line down to the 40 feet plot. Draw a line to the right and intercept the 5Amp line that comes down from the right. Where the

two line intercept, draw a line straight down, this would mean the minimum wire AWG is 20.

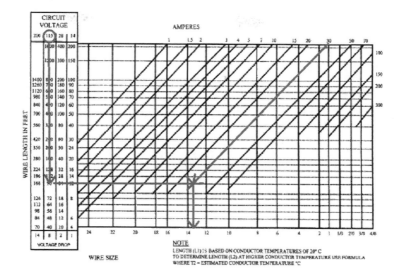

13. Starting at the 115Vac column draw a line down to the 96 feet plot. Draw a line to the right and intercept the 30Amp line that comes down from the right. Where the two lines intercept, draw a line straight down, this would mean the minimum wire AWG is 12. Remember you always want to use the next larger gauge.

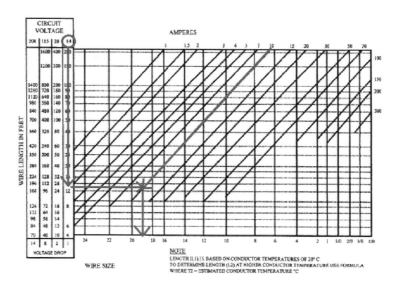

14. Starting at the 14Vdc column draw a line down to the 10 feet plot. Draw a line to the right and intercept the 10Amp line that comes down from the right. Where the two lines intercept, draw a line straight down, this would mean the minimum wire AWG is 18. Remember you always want to use the next larger gauge.

Worksheet 54

Chapter 5, Section 2

1. Three types of working drawings used in the aviation industry are Detail, Assembly and Installation

2. There are numerous salient lines used in these drawings that identify the unique details of the drawings. Each line can be described in the legend and the engineer's description that are sometimes included that can clarify some non-standard elements.

3. Section line is an index that represents various materials used in a drawing in a cross section view.

4. Three View Drawings - This drawing is used to show a 3-D representation of a product. This could be used to show; overall length, height and width.

5. Blueprints are traditional drawings that are produced from regular black line on white paper. The process is nothing more than making a negative using the original drawing. This was a method for making duplicates before copiers were available. Today these technical drawings are reproduced using much less costly methods.

6. Detail Drawings – This style drawing contains all of the required features and dimensions of parts, materials, finishes and special treatments. This is enough information to produce the part to specification.

7. Assembly drawings depict the relationship between two or more parts. These drawings reference individual parts by their part number and specify the type and number of fasteners needed to join them.

8. Installation drawing – Installation drawings contain all subassemblies that are shown in their relative position in an exploded view. They also contain a bill of materials, dimensions for adjustment, and fasteners needed to complete the installation.

9. Sectional drawing- Sectional drawing views are used when; internal construction or shape cannot be seen by viewing the part directly. This type of drawing is helpful in determining the function of a part.

10. Exploded View Drawings. Exploded view drawings are common in Illustrated Parts Catalogs (IPC) while assembly drawings are used in Maintenance Manuals. Some manufacturers use the same drawings for both publications.

Worksheet 55

Chapter 5, Section 3

1. Block diagrams use named blocks connected by lines to show relationships to components in the drawing. This type of diagram shows the communication path between the blocks.

2. Block diagrams can display as many connections that are required to show electrical, hydraulic or pneumatic paths between blocks.

3. Flow charts are used where a set path is followed to its conclusion where intermediate decision steps might be required. Flow charts can be equally useful for troubleshooting an aircraft system, or even tracking a part into a repair facility process.

4. Logic Diagrams are similar to flow charts in that the reader would have a starting point and then based on inputs sent to an outcome. The main difference is flow charts keep to a pass or fail, up or down outcome where a logic chart outcome is determined by the circuitry of the logic chart. An example is an "AND" logic requires all inputs to be 1 before it gives a 1 output and an "OR" circuit requires a 1 on either input to to give a 1 output, etc.

5. Pictorial diagrams provide simplified schematic using drawings of the actual components in the diagram along with the electrical connections between them. System descriptions in a pilots operating handbook has many of these types of drawings.

6. System schematics are very similar to electrical schematics except the flow of fluids or mechanical motion will be shown.

7. Electrical Schematics are consistent to the level of detail required by the system or component being shown. If it is shown as an aircraft radio system, the schematic will show the receiver transmitters as a block, while a schematic of a radio will show the individual components inside the radio.

8. Air Transport Wiring Diagrams have a chapter that will describe in detail the legend used in creating the schematics. This manual will describe the identification of plugs and receptacles, the method of wire identification, a description of how to locate the various components, color code options and how to use color codes.

9. In an ATA wiring diagram, the twisted shielded wires are shown as having a figure 8 around one end of the wire.

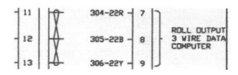

10. For an ATA wire number each is section into:1 the bundle numbers, 2 individual wire numbers, 3 wire description such as size and color coding if appropriate.

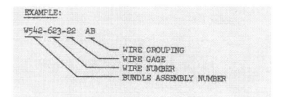

11. Power sources for GA aircraft are essentially 12 or 24 volt systems and large aircraft have 24V DC, 28V AC, 115VAC at 400 cycle and 3 phase 400 cycle 208 VAC.

12. After generation the power is fed into a common distribution bar or cable called a bus.

13. GA aircraft normally will use the power type supplied to for all of the components in the aircraft. Air Carrier aircraft because of different load requirements of the systems will need to convert the voltage that is produced from the generators.

Worksheet 56

Chapter 5, Section 2

1. The relay for the landing light system is normally open.
2. The motor uses a center tapped field winding that will drive the motor in opposite directions.
3. When the light is retracted the relay for the light and the retract micro-switch are open.
4. The switch in the cockpit is a single pole double throw (SPDT)
5. As the extend switch is placed to the extend position, power travel immediately from the landing light relay.
6. For the light to illuminate the relay must be energized and the light must have moved far enough to make contact with the contact bar.
7. You know that a part is mechanically connected when the drawing included a dashed line between the two movable components.
8. Power for the magnetic brake must come through the brushes and the armature windings through the micro switches.
9. The motor for this system is series wound.
10. If the voltage is leaving the relay there needs to be voltage past the extend microswitch.
11. If everything is working then the light the most oblivious item to check.
12. When the light drives to the extend position, it relies on the opening of the extend microswitch to open and remove power from the motor. If the motor reaches its limits and does not power down, the motor will pop the breaker.

13. Power for the retract motor must pass through the retract microswitch. Moving the switch to retract removes power from the light relay but the motor should drive.

Worksheet 57
Chapter 6, Section 1

1. Electrical shock and physical burns are the main two causes of work place deaths each year.

2. Electrical burns are caused by the flow of electricity with a high enough amperes to cause high resistance and therefore enough heat to burn flesh and skin.

3. The severity of an injury to a body depends on; the path through which current flows, the amount of amperes and the duration of the shock through the body.

4. Burns are the most common shock-related injuries because most injuries occur to extremities and are usually of a short duration.

5. The danger of having a low rated circuit breaker is that the wires will fail and burn before the maximum rated current is reached for the breaker.

6. The most found OSHA violations in the work place are improper grounding of electrical equipment.

7. A GFI uses the ratio of current coming out of a device with the current going to. This provides a fast indication of a fault because if a unit is malfunctioning, a large load will be used at the device and little to no load will return to the circuit.

8. If a GFI trips continuously during operation, some of the load for the device is going someplace other than the tools circuit.

9. When working on an electrical system on an aircraft, the technician needs to tell others that they need power off to a certain system. This can be done pulling the breakers and switches and danger tagging and documenting those systems

Worksheet 58
Chapter 6, Section 1

1. Protective footwear for avionic technicians should also protect against electrical shocks by having a sole with high resistance.

2. The first priority for any technician is to remove electrical power from any system they are intending to work on.

3. Hard hats should protect from falling objects but also from electrical shocks. This means that metal hard hats should never be worn around electrical equipment.

4. Electro Static Discharge is uncontrolled static discharges through electrical components that could damage sensitive components.

5. ESD is a concern to technicians because they are in a position to be removing, replacing and performing maintenance on equipment were improper grounding causes damage deep inside the components.

6. There only needs to be a discharge of around 100 volts to damage microprocessors.

7. Upset damage may be so small that the only ill effects could be to computer processing and simple functions. Sometime reloading software may need to be done to repair the damage.

8. Latent damage may go unnoticed and the unit might pass a BITE test but damage may be severe enough to totally damage a function of the box not tested in the BITE.

9. Catastrophic failures are seen by the technician immediately and the unit will not pass a BITE test.

10. A technician needs to be electrically grounded both on their person through wrist straps at the work station but also needs to be foot grounded to reduce the static charges that can build up when walking from station to station.

11. A dissipative workstation is a conductive work surface that is grounded so that when a component under test is placed on it, the static charges will conduct away from the unit under test through the chassis.

12. A Material Safety Data Sheet is a document that describes all of the hazardous and personal safety information required for the safe use and handling of a HAZMATs.

13. A HAZMAT is any material that meets government standards for Toxically levels, if they exceed a Threshold Limit for hygiene and if the compound is found to have cancer causing, corrosive, irritant or causes damage to specific organs.

14. A copy of the MSDS document should be kept with safety and emergency response personnel at the facility and a copy should be in the area were the individual technician works with the compound.

15. Before actually handling any HAZMAT a technician needs to know:

    a. The PPE required for handling the material
    b. The procedures for accidental exposure
    c. The storage and disposition of the material

Worksheet 59
Chapter 7, Section 1

1. The Wright brothers discovered the flight controls needed to fly their aircraft.

2. The movement about the lateral axis is called the pitch axis.

3. The Wright brothers used a forward mounted elevator called a canard because of its location.

4. The Wright brothers used wing warping to achieve the roll movement.

5. The rudder is used to effect a yawing action around the vertical axis.

6. Adverse yaw is caused by ailerons rolling the aircraft for a turning movement by the downward directed aileron creating drag.

7. Overcoming adverse yaw is accomplished by deflecting the rudder in the direction of the turn.

Worksheet 60
Chapter 7, Section 1

1. The forces acting on an aircraft in stable flight are Lift, Drag, Thrust, and Gravity.

2. The accelerated molecules of air caused by the camber on the top of the wing lowers the pressure.

3. The upper camber of the wing is the contoured surface forming the top of the wing measured from the center leading edge to the trailing edge of the wing.

4. The angle of attack is the measured angle between the chord line of the wing and the direction of the relative wind of the aircraft in flight.

5. The wing will develop additional lift and cause the aircraft to climb.

6. Increasing the angle of attack beyond the normal operating envelope of the aircraft, the wing will stall and lose all lift.

7. Thrust is derived by the engine in the aircraft and in typically GA aircraft use internal combustion reciprocating engines.

8. Parasite drag which is caused by all of the bits and pieces on the aircraft, i.e. landing gears, struts, etc. and induced drag, which is directly proportional to the aircraft speed.

9. Induced drag is inversely proportional to airspeed, meaning that as airspeed increases the induced drag will decrease.

10. Wing loading is the amount of weight a wing can support per square feet. To obtain the wing loading you divide the total square footage of the wing surface into the gross weight.

11. Wingtip vortices are caused by high pressure passing from the bottom of the wing to the upper surface of the wing at the wingtips, causing a rotating vortex that trails the wing, that increases drag.

12. The solution to control wingtip vortices has been by installing winglets on the wingtips to slow or stop the rotating of the vortex.

Worksheet 61

Chapter 7, Section 1
1. The ailerons are mounted on outer trailing edge of the wing and they operate differentially as when one goes up the other goes down.

2. The fuselage is the part of the aircraft that the wings and empennage are attached to and the cockpit and passenger compartments are contained in.

3. The wings are designed to carry the entire weight of the aircraft in a wide range of airspeeds.

4. The empennage includes the vertical and horizontal stabilizers and the rudder and elevator.

5. The rudder and elevators move with the primary flight control.

6. The flaps are mounted on the inboard trailing edge part of the wing

7. The flaps increase the area of the wing and provide additional lift to allow for slower flight during the landing mode.

8. Landing gear classified as either fixed or retractable.

9. The rudder controls the aircraft around the yaw axis and corrects for adverse yaw.

10. The elevator controls the aircraft in the pitch axis.

Worksheet 62
Chapter 7, Section 1

1. The primary controls are those that directly move an aircraft about the three axis.

2. The lift augmenting devices are the trailing edge flaps and the leading edge slats and flaps.

3. Aircraft spoilers in large aircraft have two purposes, one to spoil the airflow of the wing and at the same time increasing drag. The second is to help an aircraft turn at high control inputs without adversely affecting the yaw of the aircraft.

4. As the flaps extend behind the wings, the wing area increases which will increase lift of the wing. This also increases the induced drag.

5. The flaps allow the aircraft to fly slower by lowering the wing loading and also increase the descent angle to the runway thereby lowering the nose and allowing the pilots to have better visibility over the nose on approach.

6. The slotted flaps allow the air to flow over and on top of the flaps to allow them to maintain their laminar flow. This reduces drag and buffeting while increasing lift at lower airspeeds.

7. With the addition of slats and flaps, the wings overall upper camber is greatly increased therefore, increasing the overall wing area which will reduce the wing loading.

8. A Kruger leading edge flap is one that actually folds out from under the leading edge dramatically changing the camber providing higher wing area and therefore greater lift.

9. The two types of spoilers are the flight and ground spoilers. The ground spoilers only operate on the ground to help the aircraft decreasing the lift and putting more weight on the wheels for increased braking action. The flight spoilers assist by rapidly reducing lift causing the aircraft to slow and descend at a high rate without over speeding They also assist the aileron control at higher control inputs to achieve rapid roll rates.

Worksheet 63
Chapter 7, Section 1

1. The purpose of a trim system is to relieve flight control pressures required to maintain aircraft balance in flight caused by changes in attitude, airspeed and configuration.

2. A trim tab is mounted to the trailing edge of the flight control which in turn will move the flight control effecting the trim action.

3. If the trim tab is moved up into the wind this forces the elevator control down which in turn will pitch the nose of the aircraft down.

4. A bungee cord attached to a trim lever will reset the neutral position of the flight control surface. In other words, the bungee will provide tension on the flight control to assist the pilot in low powered aircraft and gliders.

5. A trim system is usually actuated in an aircraft either manually with a cable or gear or electrically with bi-directional motors.

6. Large aircraft have adjustable stabilizers that move the entire horizontal stabilizer to reconfigure the aircraft.

7. Air carrier electrical trim systems have two switches that have to be actuated at the same time to prevent inadvertent trim movement.

Worksheet 64
Chapter 7, Section 1

1. There are three classifications of aircraft stability, neutral, positive and negative.

2. This is an example of negative stability where when upset the aircraft will increase its rate of deflection in the direction of deflection.

3. For most aircraft designs, a positive stability is desired so if the aircraft attitude is upset it will return back to level flight.

4. When a stabilizer is placed aft of the center of balance, whenever the aircraft attitude is upset, the stabilizer shows more surface to the wind and forces the aircraft to return to a neutral position.

5. Lateral stability is about the aircrafts roll axis.

6. Aircraft wings will have dihedral built into them to allow them to right themselves when upset.

7. Longitudinal stability is designed into aircraft by adding down force to the tail.

8. As an aircraft's airspeed increases the down force on the tail increases, which in turn will cause the nose of the aircraft to rise, slowing the aircraft returning the balance.

9. In GA aircraft, the propeller causes the most left turning tendencies.

Worksheet 65
Chapter 7, Section 1

1. Aircraft designers need to balance between lightweight and strength when making aircraft.

2. Primary structure is that part, that the failure of, would cause a catastrophic failure to the aircraft.

3. Early aircraft used trussed construction which had the wings externally braced structure.

4. A full monocoque fuselage is one that whose strength is attributed to the skins providing all of the structural integrity. Design considerations such as doors windows and other fittings; prevent a true monocoque construction in aircraft.

5. When a structure needs a single strut or brace then this design is called a semi-monocoque construction.

6. Longitudal stringers are added to the structures that run from the nose to the tail of an aircraft.

7. A bulkhead is the section that reinforces a doorway of the circumference of the fuselage.

8. The wing spar is the strongest part of the wing.

9. The nose and rear ribs in a wing help shape the airfoil of the wing.

Worksheet 66

Chapter 7, Section 1

1. Balance is important in aircraft operation because aircraft are designed so that the wing carries the majority of the weight and the flight controls move the aircraft around the wing.

2. The fulcrum in a lever is the same as the center of balance or center of gravity in an aircraft.

3. When making weight and balance calculations; the weight of the object times the arm, which is the location of the weight, will equal the overall moment. The total moment divided by the total weight is a number that represents the center of gravity in inches aft of the datum.

4. The datum is the location that all weights of an aircraft are measured from. This is usually at the firewall or at the front of the aircraft.

5. The moment is a number that is the multiple of the arm, which is the distance from the datum of the equipment, times weight of all of the equipment installed in the aircraft.

6. The total moment is calculated by adjusting all of the moments of all of the equipment being installed or removed in the aircraft.

7. Center of Gravity is then calculated by dividing the total moment by the total weight of the aircraft.

8. The center of gravity is a number in inches from the aircraft datum point.

9. The whole aircraft can be placed on scales and the sum of the three weights of each scale multiplied by the arm. The addition of the three moments then divided by the total weight gives a new CG number. If the aircraft is being heavily modified, the technician may what to weight the whole aircraft.

10. The aircrafts weight and balance section in the aircraft flight manual (AFM) and aircraft maintenance records must show the new empty CG.

11. The CG range is the computed CG that is a distance from the datum where an aircraft can be loaded and the aircraft can be expected to operate safely. The CG range is specified by the type certificate data sheet.

12. In an aft CG operation, the aircraft may not enough have enough lifting force on the tail to be able to lower the nose in order to allow the recovery from a slow

speed stall. If the aft CG is exceeded for the loading conditions, the normal horizontal down force may be too high for the pilot to recover from a nose high attitude.

13. Solve for new CG after a motor installation.

	Weight	CG	Total Moment
Empty Weight	1,683	39.7	66,815

Installation of new motor: location from Datum - 117.00 inches
Weight of new motor - 5.4 lbs

Determine Arm for Motor
$5.4 \times 117.00 = 631.8$

Add new weight
1683
+ 5.4
1688

Add New Moment
66815
+ 632
67447

Determine New CG
$\frac{67447}{1688} = 39.9$ inches

Worksheet 67
Chapter 7, Section 2

1. Metal can begin corroding by chemical contaminates or electrochemical attacks.

2. Electrolytes are electrically conductive solutions that cause current to flow on metal surfaces.

3. There four major types of corrosion that affect aircraft structures.

4. Metals that are alloyed have entirely crystalline structures made up of grains.

5. When an electrolyte is present, electrons will flow from a region of cathodic to anodic.

6. Metals that lose electrons easily are susceptible to corrosion damage more than noble metals are.

7. Acids are the most corrosive agent to bare metal.

8. Alkalis are the opposite of acids in that they neutralize the etching effects of acids. But alkalis by themselves are still corrosive because they will still provide an electrolytic path on the metal.

9. Surface corrosion is called uniform etch and is seen as a uniform dulling of a surface that then progresses into deeper etching over time.

10. When tiny holes or pits become present after cleaning a corroded surface, this is an indication of pitting damage.

11. Crevice cell corrosion can be found in faying surfaces where through capillary action moisture can be trapped.

12. Galvanic corrosion is caused by two dissimilar metals in contact in an electrolytic solution.

13. Intergranular corrosion is found deep in metal grains that affect the structural strength of the metal.

14. For corrosion to be stopped the flow of electrons on the surface need to be stopped.

Worksheet 68
Chapter 7, Section 3

1. The FAA will issue a Standard Airworthiness Certificate if an aircraft meets the airworthiness standards.

2. A type design is where the aircraft meets the requirements for certain Federal Air Regulations.

3. FAR Part 23 are the type design standards for small general aviation aircraft.

4. Instructions for continued airworthiness include all data required to maintain and repair an aircraft, to include the maintenance and service manuals.

5. The Air Transport Association (ATA) developed a set of chapters to simplify the manual systems for aircraft maintenance which is universally adopted worldwide.

6. The structural repair manual describes all of the methods and techniques required for major structural repairs on air transport category aircraft.

7. When selecting the proper diagram, the technician needs to know the aircraf's effectivity number which describes the electrical component configuration in the aircraft at the time.

8. FAR 43.9 describes the content and form of maintenance records after maintenance.

9. When work is performed by a mechanic working under a FAR 145 repair station certificate, the name of the mechanic is signed with the number of the repair station.

10. When work is performed by an un-certificated mechanic, both the un-certificated mechanic who performed the maintenance, and the certificated mechanic who supervised the work, names must be entered in the maintenance record.

11. When there is a reference to approved data, this implies that the data has been approved by the FAA or by some other FAA approved process.

12. The FAA will issue an Airworthiness Directive which will require immediate action before the aircraft can be considered airworthy.

13. A service bulletin is a safety issue or product improvement that the manufacturer feels that needs attention; however an AD is where the FAA will review a service bulletin and decide that an Airworthiness Directive may need to be issued right away.

14. For major repairs or alterations to aircraft, the work needs to be documented on an FAA Form 337 and sent to the FAA for approval.

15. Examples of acceptable data for repair or alteration that can be used on an FAA Form 337 are:
   a. Manufacturers Maintenance Manual
   b. Service Bulletins
   c. Airworthiness Directive
   d. Supplemental Type Certificates (STC)

16. If a technician desires to use acceptable data for installation of a major repair or alteration from a different aircraft, the technician can apply for field approval of the data from the FAA.

Worksheet 69
Chapter 7, Section 4
   1. A technician needs to understand fully the proper operation of a system before determining what, if anything is malfunctioning.

   2. One of the first steps in the troubleshooting process to ensure electrical power for the system is available.

3. If the system will not turn on with the proper switches, then check the circuit breakers for electrical power.

4. Most modern aircraft systems have self-test systems called BITE (Built In Test Equipment) checks.

5. The simplest piece of test equipment is the multimeter.

6. A multimeter is designed to measure, DC Voltage, AC Voltage, Resistance, and Amperes or current flow.

7. Most modern multimeters can make simple tests of diodes by measuring the forward bias.

8. An ammeter is connected in a circuit in series, in which you would disconnect the section to be tested and connect the red lead to the power supply side and the black to the load side.

9. An ammeter shunt is an internal conductor in a meter with a precise resistance value. A voltmeter is placed across the shunt to read voltage drop. The voltage drop will be converted and then displayed as amperes. This arrangement allows large current flows to be measured.

10. When connecting a voltmeter across a device in a circuit, the meter will indicate the voltage drop between the leads.

11. When connecting a voltmeter across an open fuse, the source voltage will be indicated because the meter is actually measuring from the source voltage to the ground or negative position.

12. The unit to be measured needs to be completely isolated from all other parts of the circuit when using an ohmmeter.

Worksheet 70

Chapter 7, Section 4

1. An oscilloscope is a device that is designed to plot the amplitude and frequency of a signal onto a graphic display.

2. The oscilloscope will plot the Y axis which is the amplitude of a signal and the X axis which is the time or frequency of the signal.

3. A typical oscilloscope will have an 8x10 grid marked on the face.

4. The white line on the oscilloscope page is called the trace.

5. This is a sine wave.

6. A pulse or trigger is a non-rhythmic signal that can be shown on an oscilloscope.

7. The Y-POS knob moves the trace up or down to align with a grid line.

8. This trace is too compressed over time; adjust the Time/Div knob to show a single wave form.

9. A calibrated signal generator can be connected to the second channel of the O-scope to use as comparison for calibration.

10. This is where a technician uses one lead connected to the board's chassis ground and holds the positive lead to areas on the board to be tested.

Worksheet 71
Chapter 7, Section 4

1. Resistors usually fail from overload which can create a short in the resistor or a complete open.

2. Resistors can be measured in a circuit by using a voltmeter to measure the voltage drop across the resistor.

3. Resistors are measured out of a circuit with an ohmmeter.

4. When using a multimeter to measure the function, first connect the negative lead to the cathode and the positive to the anode. Current should flow and the multimeter will beep or show no resistance. Reverse the leads and the resistance should be very high.

5. You can use a multimeter by first applying a voltage from the continuity or ohmmeter to charge the capacitor. Then set the meter to voltage and place across the leads, there should be a voltage indicated when connecting the meter.

6. A condenser tester applies a measured frequency and voltage AC signal to the capacitor, the X_C is measured. This indicates the capacitors storage ability.

7. When using a multimeter on an inductor you are measuring if the unit is either open or shorted.

8. A transformer is nothing more than two large inductors separated from each other by an air or iron core.

9. Solve for a continuity check of a transformer.

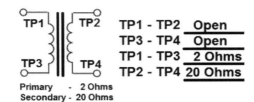

TP1 - TP2 __Open__
TP3 - TP4 __Open__
TP1 - TP3 __2 Ohms__
TP2 - TP4 __20 Ohms__

Primary   - 2 Ohms
Secondary - 20 Ohms

10. A low resistance between TP3 and TP4 indicates a short between the primary and the secondary coils.

11. Infinity would indicate an open in the secondary windings.

12. Relays will have one control circuit and one or more contact circuits.

13. Identify the circuits of a relay.

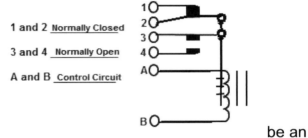

1 and 2 __Normally Closed__

3 and 4 __Normally Open__

A and B __Control Circuit__

14. An open between A and B would be an indication of an open in the coil of the control circuit.

15. High resistance on a set of contacts is an indication of dirty or burned contact surface.

Worksheet 72
Chapter 7, Section 4

1. TP1 to TP10 ___180V___

2. TP2 to TP5 ___60V___

3. TP3 to TP14 ___180V___

4. TP4 to TP7 ___0V___

5. TP1 to TP12 ___180V___

6. TP7 to TP14 ___120V___

7. TP5 to TP11 ___120V___

8. TP9 to TP10 ___120V___

9. TP13 to TP12 ___180V___

Worksheet 73

Chapter 7, Section 5

1. The purpose of a hammer is to bend or form metal while mallets are usually softer and designed to only slightly bend or move components.

2. The Reed & Prince screwdriver is a cross point tip that is constructed to a fine tip. The Phillips is also a cross point tip however the cross has a round relief in the center to allow for an easier fit.

3. Phillip screwdrivers are sized by numbers with 1 being the smallest and 4 being largest.

4. A high torque bit is designed to have a rounded bottom to fit down into a fastener.

5. A speed handle is shaped like a hand crank and can be used to turn fasteners in and out quickly.

6. Aircraft sockets are made of 18 point and 8 point types and they can be deep or shallow.

7. Use a deep socket to remove a nut off a bolt.

8. A closed head wrench is also known as a box end wrench.

9. Pliers are named for the end or nose shape.

10. The fixed jaw is placed on the pulling direction for a nut, bolt or fitting.

Worksheet 74

Chapter 7, Section 5

1. Aircraft wire stripper must not damage the tinned coating of the conductor.

2. Automotive strippers are designed for single conductor wires that are a different AWG than aircraft multi-strand wires. This may cause damage to wires. Also the insulator of automotive wire is made from material that is designed to tear while aircraft insulation needs to be cut cleanly all around the wire.

3. An automatic stripper is one that will hold, cut and release the tool with one motion of the grip.

4. Aircraft quality wire strippers will be constructed to a MIL-SPEC and it will be marked as such.

5. Automotive crimpers cannot: give a consistent crimp, cannot fit aircraft type splices in the tool, cannot crimp around the crimp evenly.

6. Aircraft crimps perform two crimps at once, one on the conductor and the other that crimps the insulation.

7. A red crimp is for AWG 22 – 16 wires.

8. For a red/blue crimper, the number of conductors that are going to be crimped at once must be set on the tool.

9. A MOLEX style connector is one that uses a mechanical crimp contact that can be inserted into plastic block connectors.

10. MOLEX contacts have two crimps done at the same time, one for the conductor and the other that crimps the insulator to provide strain relief.

11. The three parts of a MOLEX contact are the crimp section, the transition section and the mating section.

12. MOLEX connectors are found in the back of radio racks in GA aircraft.

13. MOLEX connectors use a piece of plastic inserted into the connector called a key to prevent an improper radio from being inserted.

14. Cannon style plugs are weather and chemical resistant which allows them to be used in external sections of an aircraft.

15. Cannon plugs use sockets (female) and pins (male) to make their electrical connections.

16. Cannon plugs are classified as receptacles (fixed) or plugs (removable).

17. The letters I, J, O or Q are not used because of how difficult these numbers are to read in a small connector.

18. Cannon plug contacts are color coded to identify their part numbers.

19. Crimpers for Cannon plugs must be able to produce a consistent, strong crimp that does not deform the crimp so it would jam into the connector.

20. For a Red/White connector tool, the colored end is used for insertion of the contact into the connector.

Worksheet 75

Chapter 7, Section 5

1. In aircraft, fasteners are subjected to vibration, heat and stress that might loosen or cause the fastener to disconnect from critical systems and controls.

2. Only use soft wire such as copper or soft aluminum wire that is designed to break away easily when needed.

3. The double twist method is the most common for widely spaced nuts and bolts.

4. The single wire method is used for closely spaced fasteners.

5. A .032 inch minimum diameter safety wire should be used for parts that have a hole diameter larger than 0.045 inch.

6. For a three screw head pattern the double safety wire should look like this.

7. Three bolts should be safety in this method.

EXAMPLE 3

8. Cotter pins must have a bolt with a hole in the shaft and a castle type nut.

9. To prevent injury, the ends of the cotter pin need to be trimmed in a way that would not leave a sharp edge.

10. The cotter pin needs to be snug to the shank of the bolt and the pins bent flush against the nut without touching the washer.

End

Back of the book

Bruce Bessette

Bruce is a NCATT Senior Instructor who has over 30 years of avionics and maintenance experience. He received his initial avionics training while serving in the US Air Force and went on to work in the field of Air Carrier Avionics at America West Airlines and later became an A&P Mechanic and Aircraft Inspector at Southwest Airlines. After Southwest Airlines he worked for the Federal Aviation Administration as an Aviation Safety Inspector.

After retiring from the FAA he became an instructor at Pima Community College in Tucson, AZ and developed all of the study materials and labs for the Avionics Program. In the six years since the Avionics program began, Bruce has written five text books and developed numerous avionics courses. The books include a NCATT AET review text and companion workbook.

Bruce holds an FAA A&P certificate with Inspection Authorization. For Avionics he has an FCC GROL, NCATT AET, and a NCATT Master Instructor Certificate. He has a degree in Aviation Maintenance Technology. He holds FAA pilot's certificates with Commercial Instrument with both SEL and MEL with ratings for gliders and the Boeing 737 type rating. Bruce travels all over the country providing avionics training to both new and experienced technicians and mechanics in preparing them to take the NCATT AET and is starting to Teach courses for the NCATT add on ratings.

Lorence Bessette

Larry assisted in the writing of this book by providing editing and information that helps make this book as complete as it became. He worked over 20 years in the Air Carrier industry in both engineering and maintenance. Then went to the FAA and retired after 26 years finishing his career at FAA Headquarters as the Manager of the Avionics and Repair Station Branch. He was an integral part of the transitioning of the aviation industry to the new avionics found on most aircraft today. Larry is an A&P mechanic with an IA and holds a FCC GROL. He also received the Charles Taylor Mechanics Award from the FAA to honor his over 50 years in aviation. He a pilot and has owned three aircraft. He holds Associate Degrees in Electronics and Welding and a BS in Business Administration in the field of Economics from Arizona State University.

Other books available from BCS at
www.avionicseducation.com :

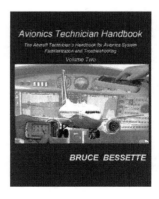